AA

D0776334

50 Walks in
DEVON

First published 2001
Researched and written by Sue Viccars

Produced by AA Publishing
© Automobile Association Developments Limited 2001
Illustrations © Automobile Association Developments Limited 2001
Reprinted 2002

Published by AA Publishing (a trading name of Automobile
Association Developments Limited, whose registered office is
Millstream, Maidenhead Road, Windsor, SL4 5GD;
registered number 1878835)

ISBN 0 7495 2872 9

A CIP catalogue record for this book is available
from the British Library.

Visit the AA Publishing website at www.theAA.com

Paste-up and editorial by Outcrop Publishing Services
for AA Publishing

Colour reproduction by LC Repro
Printed and bound by G. Canale & C. s.p.a., Torino, Italy

A01309

Legend & map

Legend

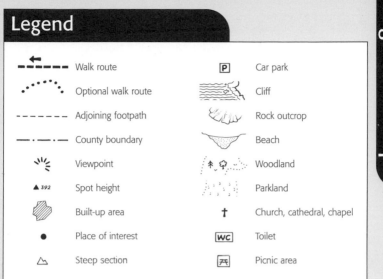

← – – – – – –	Walk route	P	Car park
••••••	Optional walk route	≈≈≈	Cliff
– – – – – –	Adjoining footpath		Rock outcrop
– · – · –	County boundary		Beach
☼	Viewpoint	♠ ♣	Woodland
▲ 392	Spot height		Parkland
	Built-up area	†	Church, cathedral, chapel
●	Place of interest	WC	Toilet
△	Steep section	🏓	Picnic area

Devon locator map

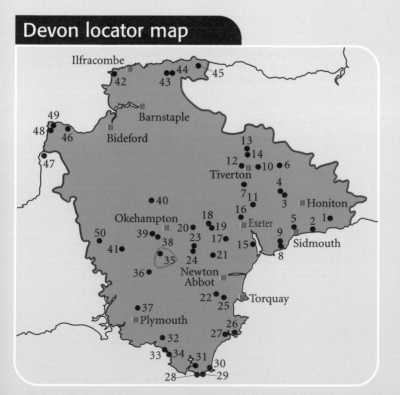

Contents

Contents

Rating: Each walk is rated for its relative difficulty compared to the other walks in this book. Walks marked 🚶🚶 🚶 🚶 are likely to be shorter and easier with little total ascent. The hardest walks are marked 🚶🚶 🚶🚶 🚶🚶 .

Walking in Safety: For advice and safety tips ➤ 128.

Introducing Devon

Devon's got it all. Surely no other county in the country has such a variety of landscapes waiting to be explored, from the comfortable, rolling, red-earth farmland of East Devon, and the deeply wooded river valleys and granite-studded wilds of Dartmoor, to the rocky coast and safe sandy coves of the South Hams. Then there's the huge expanse of relatively unexplored undulating countryside north of Dartmoor, the land of the Taw and Torridge rivers, culminating in the unforgiving cliffs – some of the highest in the country – overlooking the Bristol Channel. It's a big county too, second only in size to North Yorkshire, so there's masses for the inquisitive walker to investigate. This satisfying range of scenery, along with a welcoming population, picturesque cob-and-thatch villages, ancient stone-built churches, characterful pubs, deeply banked lanes smothered with wild flowers and an equable maritime climate combine to make Devon one of the most popular holiday destinations in the British Isles.

'Devon' is thought to derive from a Celtic tribal name, meaning 'the people of the land', and it is certainly true that those born in Devonshire are extremely proud of their roots. Those who move away tend to gravitate back to their birthplace sooner rather than later. Devon has a way of getting under the skin, and the range of walks described in this book, designed to suit every requirement from an easy farmland stroll to a tough coastal tramp, aim to show you just what a special county it is.

There are gentle ambles along riversides and canal tow paths for those who want to while away a peaceful summer afternoon among the dragonflies and waterlilies. You can take a long, yet easy, route across the border into Somerset, and investigate the lovely Blackdown Hills of East Devon, learning about the fascinating 19th-century whetstone industry there. Spend an afternoon exploring Regency Sidmouth, or Elizabethan Totnes, or wander south along the tranquil River Dart (described by Queen Victoria as 'the most beautiful stretch of any river in England'). Further south, at the mouth of the Dart, lies historic Dartmouth with its superbly situated 15th-century castle, and to the east and west walks along the undulating South West Coast Path lead to tucked-away coves and estuaries rarely visited even by those who live in the county.

And then there's Dartmoor, southern England's greatest wilderness, rising to 2,037ft (621m) and home to all manner of spine-chilling legends, not to mention holding the best evidence

---

PUBLIC TRANSPORT ⓘ

Regular public transport isn't one of the county's strongpoints, and in the more remote areas you can wait for a bus for a couple of days! None of the walks described therefore relies upon public transport, and the linear ones are 'there-and-back' walks, though a straightforward alternative return route has been described where possible. You can get bus information on (01392) 382800 for the south of the county and (01271) 382800 for the north. Local travel enquiries can also be made to traveline (0870) 6082608 or on the internet at www.pti.org.uk.

of Bronze Age habitation in Europe. But even the highest parts of Dartmoor are relatively accessible, providing you keep an eye on the weather and don't walk if there is any danger of mist. There are routes here that will introduce you to the very heart of the moor and give you an insight into its social and industrial history. By contrast there are explorations of the beautiful rocky, wooded stream-filled valleys that fringe the moor, of chocolate-box villages such as Lustleigh, and of mysterious granite formations such as the Dewerstone with its infamous

links to the Devil. Turning north you can follow part of the Tarka Trail through the little-visited heartland north of the moor, and then try some tough routes along the cliffs of the North Devon coast, culminating in the hardest walk in the book, which takes in rugged Hartland Point with its glorious views across the water to Lundy Island.

Using this Book

Information panels

An information panel for each walk shows its relative difficulty (➤ 5), the distance and total amount of ascent. An indication of the gradients you will encounter is shown by the rating ⛰️⛰️⛰️ (no steep slopes) to ⛰️⛰️⛰️ (several very steep slopes).

Maps

There are 30 maps, covering 40 of the walks. Some walks have a suggested option in the same area. The information panel for these walks will tell you how much extra walking is involved. On short-cut suggestions the panel will tell you the total distance if you set out from the start of the main walk. Where an option returns to the same point on the main walk, just the distance of the loop is given. Where an option leaves the main walk at one point and returns to it at another, then the distance shown is for the whole walk. The minimum time suggested is for reasonably fit walkers and doesn't allow for stops. Each walk has a suggested map. Laminated aqua3 maps are longer lasting and water resistant.

Start Points

The start of each walk is given as a six-figure grid reference prefixed by two letters indicating which 100km square of the National Grid it refers to. You'll find more information on grid references on most Ordnance Survey maps.

Dogs

We have tried to give dog owners useful advice about how dog friendly each walk is. Please respect other countryside users. Keep your dog under control, especially around livestock, and obey local bylaws and other dog control notices.

Car Parking

Many of the car parks suggested are public, but occasionally you may find you have to park on the roadside or in a lay-by. Please be considerate when you leave your car, ensuring that access roads or gates are not blocked and that other vehicles can pass safely.

The River Coly and the Umborne Brook

The tranquil East Devon town of Colyton has a chequered history.

•DISTANCE•	4¼ miles (7km)
•MINIMUM TIME•	2hrs 30min
•ASCENT / GRADIENT•	197ft (60m) ▲ ▲▲
•LEVEL OF DIFFICULTY•	🚶 🚶 🚶
•PATHS•	Fields and country lanes, one narrow boggy track, 9 stiles
•LANDSCAPE•	Level river meadows and rolling farmland
•SUGGESTED MAP•	aqua3 OS Explorer 116 Lyme Regis & Bridport
•START / FINISH•	Grid reference: SY 245940
•DOG FRIENDLINESS•	Livestock in some fields
•PARKING•	Paying car park in centre of Colyton (Dolphin Street)
•PUBLIC TOILETS•	At car park

BACKGROUND TO THE WALK

In some ways the pretty East Devon town of Colyton is a rather misleading place. Situated in rolling countryside on the banks of the River Coly, the town has more than once won 'the prettiest village in Devonshire' accolade. The narrow, winding streets, attractive cottages, with hanging baskets and colourful gardens, give no clues as to why Colyton was once dubbed 'most rebellious town in Devon'. For this we must go back to the 1600s. The town supported Parliament in the Civil War in 1643, and was the scene of many skirmishes against Royalists based at Axminster. It also played a part in the Monmouth Rebellion of 1685, when over 100 Colyton men – more than anywhere else in Devon – joined the Duke of Monmouth's army. Monmouth landed at Lyme Regis with 80 followers, managed to raise an army of 3,000, but was defeated by James II's army at Sedgemoor near Bridgwater in Somerset. In the trials that followed, the 'Bloody Assizes', 17 Colyton men were hanged, and 18 were transported to the West Indies. Only two of the latter made it back to Devon.

But Colyton's history hasn't always been so colourful. There is evidence of prehistoric occupation – a Pleistocene flint axe as well as Bronze and Iron Age remains have been found locally. The Romans were here from around AD 70, but Colyton is essentially a Saxon town. Egbert, King of Wessex, held a parliament here in AD 827 and a fine restored 9th-century cross can be seen in the church. The town developed into one of Devon's major commercial centres, its wealth based on weaving cloth, silk and serge, and lacemaking. Many of the farms you'll pass on this walk have the suffix *hayne*, meaning 'enclosure', implying that they date from the 13th and 14th centuries; and in the great wool days of the 15th-century Colyton was one of the three wealthiest towns in the county.

St Andrew's Church

The parish church is prominent in the view of Colyton towards the end of the walk. It also reflects the prosperous side of the town. There has been a church here since AD 700, but the current building is based on a Norman church from the mid-12th century. The most unusual feature is the distinctive and rare octagonal lantern, set on the square Norman tower in the 15th century. This is thought to have been inspired by similar towers seen in Flanders by the town's wool merchants. There is a merchant's mark (representing a 'stapler' or wool merchant) on the floor slate marking the grave of Hugh Buckland in the chancel.

Walk 1 Directions

① From the car park turn right, then first left into **Lower Church Street**. Turn left again at the **Gerrard Arms** into **Rosemary Lane**, then right into **Vicarage Street**. Go right, towards the river, and cross the bridge.

② Turn left through a kissing gate and along the riverbank on the **East Devon Way** (EDW). Follow the path through two kissing gates.

Ignore the next footpath sign right, but go straight ahead through another two kissing gates, following the river bank.

③ At the junction of footpaths at the end of that field keep the river left and take the kissing gate in the corner ahead onto a concrete walkway. Go through a kissing gate and across a field, aiming for two kissing gates and a footbridge below three big oaks. Cross another footbridge/gate to reach a bridge over the river on the left.

④ Turn right (leaving EDW), through a gate onto a lane and turn right. After 400yds (366m) at **Cadhayne Farm** (right) turn left through the gate opposite the farmyard (the footpath sign may be overgrown). Walk steadily uphill, through the gate at the top and straight on. This green lane soon veers sharp left; turn right along a narrow, muddy path, ending at a tarmac road signed 'Tritchayne'.

WHILE YOU'RE THERE ⓘ

It's worth going to have a look at **Blackberry Camp** Iron Age hillfort, an English Heritage site signposted from the A3052 Colyton to Sidford road. Probably occupied by a cattle farming community between the 1st and 2nd centuries AD, this D-shaped enclosure, defended by a single bank and ditch, is a wonderfully peaceful spot for a picnic. It's best seen at bluebell time in May.

---

⑤ Cross over and walk downhill along **Watery Lane**. At **Tritchmarsh** the lane becomes a grassy track; follow the footpath sign right on a wooden walkway. Go sharp left to a gate and left round the field. Ignore the next stile left; take the small gate/bridge/gate to the right and cross the paddock and the **Umborne Brook** via a gate and concrete walkway to **Lexhayne Mill**. The path runs between the house and yard to a kissing gate; over the

---

WHERE TO EAT AND DRINK ⓘ

The **Old Court House tea shop** and restaurant in Queen Square has a courtyard garden today, concealing a somewhat infamous past – Judge Jeffreys tried many locals here during the Bloody Assize in 1685. The **Gerrard Arms** (Point ①) is a free house with an attractive garden, a skittle alley and a range of bar food. There is also a tea room at **Colyton Station** and several other pubs and cafés in the village.

---

stile in the wire fence (the main line railway is ahead). Cross over the next stile, then head diagonally right for the drive to **Lexhayne Farm**. Go left, then right (signed) through a hedge gap.

⑥ Cross diagonally down the field towards the bottom corner, over a double gate/bridge and the big footbridge over the brook. Walk left; over a stile, then across the brook via a double gate/footbridge with **Colyton church** ahead.

⑦ Aim for the stile in the fence ahead right. Go straight on to cross the brook via a double gate/bridge, then left. Cross a stile and two stiles/footbridges then diagonally across the upper part of the next field. Cross a stile, go downhill and over a stile onto the road.

⑧ Turn left; pass the picnic area/playground at **Road Green**, then over the bridge. Take the first left (**Vicarage Street**) and go straight on to pass the church (left), through the town centre and down **Silver Street** to the car park.

WHAT TO LOOK FOR ⓘ

Take a trip in an open-top tramcar beside the River Axe on the **Seaton Tramway**, which runs for 3 miles (4.8km) from Colyton to Seaton via Colyford. You should see a wide range of birds, including grey herons, kingfishers, oystercatchers, curlews and egrets. More than 50 different species have been spotted from the tram in one day! The tram line, the first section of which opened in 1970, utilises part of the old Seaton branch railway, which was axed by Dr Beeching and closed in 1966. The extension to Colyton opened in 1980. Trams depart every twenty minutes throughout the season (early April to the end of October), with weekend opening during November and December.

The Cliffs of East Devon

Along the coast near Branscombe – one of the longest villages in Devon.

Walk 2

•DISTANCE•	6¼ miles (10km)
•MINIMUM TIME•	3hrs 30min
•ASCENT / GRADIENT•	492ft (150m) ▲ ▲▲ ▲
•LEVEL OF DIFFICULTY•	🚶🚶 🚶🚶 🚶
•PATHS•	Coast path (one steep ascent), country lanes, 14 stiles
•LANDSCAPE•	Undulating cliffs, farmland and woodland
•SUGGESTED MAP•	aqua3 OS Explorer 115 Exeter & Sidmouth
•START / FINISH•	Grid reference: SY 167890
•DOG FRIENDLINESS•	Can be off lead but livestock in some fields
•PARKING•	Unsurfaced car park at Weston
•PUBLIC TOILETS•	Behind Branscombe village hall, also in car park at Branscombe Mouth

BACKGROUND TO THE WALK

Picturesque Branscombe, situated where three deep, wooded valleys converge, is one of the most secluded and peaceful villages in this unspoilt corner of East Devon. Groups of pretty flower-decked cottages sit either side of a long narrow lane that runs gradually down the valley from Street, giving rise to the claim that Branscombe is one of the longest villages in the county.

The Coast Path
This walk takes you to the village along the coast path from Weston. There are extensive views all along the path, and on a clear day Portland Bill can be seen to the east. The sloping grassy area on the cliff above Littlecombe Shoot is a popular spot for paragliders. If the weather conditions are favourable for flight you can spend hours sitting on the cliff top watching them soar above you. At the footpath marker post here a sign leading right appears to direct you straight over the edge of the cliff. This steep, narrow, zig-zag path will take you onto the pebbly beach below. A number of privately owned wooden chalets dot about the cliff, hiding behind straggling clumps of old man's beard: it's a wonderfully romantic spot.

St Winifred's Church nestles comfortably half-way down the valley from Street, and is one of Branscombe's treasures. Dedicated to an obscure Welsh saint, it dates from the 11th century and is significant in Devon in that it reveals evidence of continuous development up to the 16th century. The squat tower dates from Norman times. Inside there are remnants of medieval paintings that once adorned the walls, and an Elizabethan gallery. It also has an unusual 18th-century three-decker pulpit. There are many memorials to local families, including Nicholas Wadham, founder of Wadham College, Oxford. Near the village 'centre', by the village hall, many buildings are owned by the National Trust: the Old Bakery (the last traditional working bakery in Devon until 1987 – now a tea room), Manor Mill (a recently restored water-powered mill), and the Forge, complete with working blacksmith.

The beach at Branscombe Mouth gets busy in summer, although it is pebbly and the seabed shelves away quickly. This is the half-way point of the walk and you can always wander a little way to east or west to escape the crowds.

Walk 2

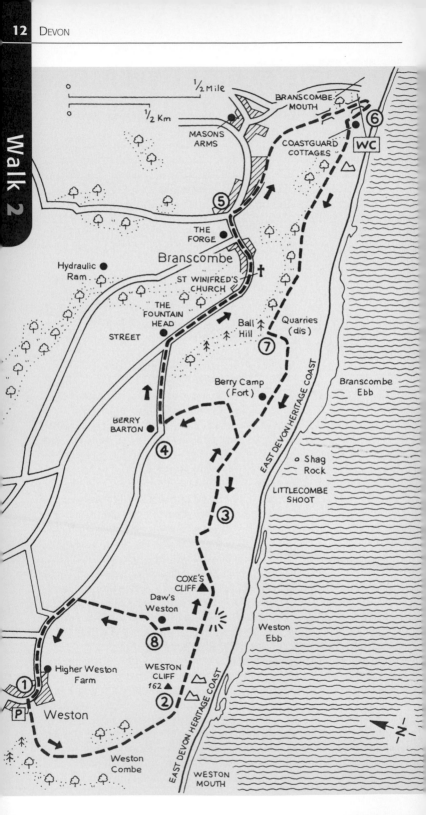

½ Mile

½ Km

BRANSCOMBE MOUTH

MASONS ARMS

COASTGUARD COTTAGES

WC

⑥

⑤

THE FORGE

Branscombe

Hydraulic Ram

ST WINIFRED'S CHURCH

THE FOUNTAIN HEAD

STREET

Ball Hill

Quarries (dis)

⑦

Berry Camp (Fort)

Branscombe Ebb

BERRY BARTON

④

EAST DEVON HERITAGE COAST

Shag Rock

LITTLECOMBE SHOOT

③

COXE'S CLIFF ▲

Daw's Weston

⑧

Weston Ebb

Higher Weston Farm

①

WESTON CLIFF
162 ▲

②

P

Weston

EAST DEVON HERITAGE COAST

Weston Combe

WESTON MOUTH

N

Walk 2 Directions

① From the car park take the flinty track over the stile onto the East Devon Heritage Coast path signposted '**Weston Mouth**'. After ½ mile (800m) the sea comes into view at a stile and gate. Go straight on, then veer left across the field to join the coast path at another stile.

② Go left, steeply uphill (wooden steps), to reach the grassy top of **Weston Cliff**. A kissing gate leads onto **Coxe's Cliff** and the path runs diagonally away from the coast via a deep combe towards another stile in the top left corner of the field. Cross the next field and stile onto grassland above **Littlecombe Shoot**.

> **WHERE TO EAT AND DRINK** ⓘ
> The 14th-century **Fountain Head** at Street brews its own beer (recommended by CAMRA), has great food and a local feel. The **Masons Arms** (hotel and restaurant) at the bottom of the valley is more upmarket but both pubs welcome families. The National Trust **Old Bakery Tearoom** can be found near Branscombe village hall, and the **Sea Shanty café** is at the beach at Branscombe Mouth.

③ Go past the coast path marker ahead to pass two stands of gorse (left). Turn diagonally left, away from the cliff, towards a banked gap in a scrubby gorse hedge. Aim for a metal gate in the top left corner of the next field, then turn left down the track to join the lane at **Berry Barton**.

④ Turn right down the lane to the **Fountain Head** pub. Turn right again down the valley, passing groups of thatched cottages and **St Winifred's Church** (right). Continue downhill past the post office and the **Forge** to **St Branoc's Well** and the village hall.

⑤ Turn right opposite **Parkfield Terrace** down the lane signposted '**Branscombe Mouth**'. After 200yds (183m) a farm gate leads to a well-signposted path through the field to a footbridge and gate (go left here for the **Masons Arms**). Go through the next meadow and gate. Turn right over a wooden bridge and gate to reach **Branscombe Mouth**.

⑥ Turn immediately right through a kissing gate to join coast path signs uphill beneath the coastguard cottages (now a private house). Go through an open gateway and left into the woods via a stile. Ignore all paths to the left and right until, after two stiles and ½ mile (800m), a signpost points left between grassy hummocks towards the cliffs.

⑦ Follow the coastal footpath signs to rejoin the cliff edge, over a stile onto **Littlecombe Shoot**. Retrace your steps over two stiles to **Coxe's Cliff**, then a stile and kissing gate onto **Weston Cliff**. Turn immediately right through a kissing gate into a wildflower meadow.

⑧ Pass the cottage and outbuildings (on the right) over two stiles and onto a track leading to a tarmac lane. Go left and in a short while you'll reach **Weston** and your car.

> **WHILE YOU'RE THERE** ⓘ
> The **Donkey Sanctuary** at Slade House Farm (signposted off the A3052) is a charity devoted to caring for donkeys that have been neglected or badly treated, or are unwanted. Founded in 1969, it's the largest donkey sanctuary in the world and looks after 600 donkeys. It's open every day of the year, admission free.

Picturesque Broadhembury

Beech woods and rolling farmland around an unspoilt thatched village.

•DISTANCE•	5½ miles (9km)
•MINIMUM TIME•	2hrs 30min
•ASCENT / GRADIENT•	360ft (110m) ▲▲ ▲▲ ▲
•LEVEL OF DIFFICULTY•	🚶🚶 🚶🚶 🚶
•PATHS•	Country lanes, pastures and woodland paths, 7 stiles
•LANDSCAPE•	Rolling farmland and beech woods
•SUGGESTED MAP•	aqua3 OS Explorer 115 Exeter & Sidmouth
•START / FINISH•	Grid reference: SY 095068
•DOG FRIENDLINESS•	Possibility of livestock in some fields
•PARKING•	Unsurfaced car park at Knowles Wood
•PUBLIC TOILETS•	By the Drewe Arms in centre of Broadhembury

BACKGROUND TO THE WALK

Broadhembury is one of those unspoilt showpiece Devon villages that gives you the impression that nothing has changed for centuries and that you've entered some sort of time warp. The picturesque main street is lined with well-preserved cob and thatched cottages and pretty flower-filled gardens, and there appears to be a constant cycle of repair and renovation going on. Much of Broadhembury as you see it today developed as an estate village under the patronage of the Drewe family in the early 17th century, and you still get the feeling that this is certainly not a village struggling for survival.

The Drewe Family

St Andrew's Church holds many memorials to members of the family, who have been highly influential in the development of the village. In 1603 Edward Drewe, Sergeant-at-Law to Queen Elizabeth I, bought Abbey Farm from Dunkeswell Abbey, and created a new mansion, The Grange, which remained the family seat for nearly 300 years. Edward Drewe was a successful lawyer, who already owned Sharpham and Killerton. The oak drawing room at The Grange is said to be one of the most beautiful in the country. The house is not open to the public, but you can get a good view of it from the south east approach road to the village.

The church was consecrated in 1259, but the building dates mainly from the 15th century, constructed of local flint and chalky limestone from Beer. It's set at the end of a cul-de-sac of chestnut trees and has been much restored over the last couple of centuries. The tower (from about 1480) is almost 100ft (30m) high. The timbers of the roof were painted in the late 15th century and were only discovered in 1930 when repair work was being carried out. There is also an unusual 15th-century font which is somewhat damaged (probably during the Civil War) and decorated with primitive figures of apostles and clergy, and an 18th-century memorial to Augustus Toplady, who wrote the hymn *Rock of Ages*.

Just a mile (1.6km) to the south east of the village lies Hembury hillfort, on a spur of the Blackdown Hills at 883ft (269m) above sea level. There was a causewayed camp here around 2500 BC, and in about 150 BC Iron Age dwellers built the defensive earthworks that can be seen today. The site was inhabited until around AD 75. The best time of year to explore the hillfort is in May, when the ramparts are smothered with a carpet of bluebells.

Walk 3

Blackborough

½ mile

0

½ Km

Newcombe Common

PONCHYDOWN

Newcombe Common

WOODLAND TRUST LAND

Forest Glade House

Knowles Wood

Downlands Plantations

Knowles House

① ▲ 283

DEVON & SOMERSET GLIDING CLUB

③

North Hill

②

⑧

BARLEYCOMBE FARM

Rifle Range

Moor Copse

Hanger Farm

⑦

R. Tale

④

Skinner's Copse

–N–

⑥

WC

THE DREWE ARMS

Broadhembury ⑤ ST ANDREWS CHURCH

Walk 3 Directions

① Return to the road and turn left uphill. Very shortly a bridleway sign points right through another parking area. After a few minutes this narrow, level path reaches a signpost and metal gate (left), indicating that you have reached the Devon & Somerset Gliding Club. Ignore the gate, continue on the bridleway.

② Pass through the next metal gate onto the airfield. Turn left along the edge, keeping to the right of the clubhouse. Follow the tarmac drive left over a cattle grid and down the lane to join a road.

WHAT TO LOOK FOR

The **Devon & Somerset Gliding Club** is near the start of the walk at Northill, over 900ft (280m) above sea level – a popular spot with skylarks, too! The return leg skirts along the edge of the airfield; the gliders are launched using a steel cable, so it's wise to keep well out of the way. There's something quite magical – and tempting – about watching the gliders drift silently through the air above you, often reaching heights of over 2,000ft (600m).

---

③ Turn right; pass **Barleycombe Farm** (on the left), then follow bridleway signs right through a gate, left through another and into a field. Follow the track along the bottom of the field. The path curves right through a stand of beech trees and a metal gate, then runs straight across the next field towards a big beech tree and gate. Take the stony track through the gate. After 100yds (91m) bear right along a grassy path (ignore the gate straight ahead) and through two metal gates, with a coniferous plantation to the right.

④ The path ends at a lane; turn right downhill into **Broadhembury**. At **St Andrew's Church** cross the road and go through the churchyard, then under the lychgate and downhill to find the **Drewe Arms** (left) for a welcome break.

⑤ To continue the walk, from the pub, turn left down the main street to reach the bridge and ford. Turn right up the lane, past the playground and up the hill.

⑥ Just past two thatched cottages go left over the stile in the hedge and up the field, aiming for a stile in the top left corner. Go over that and straight ahead, keeping the old farmhouse and barn conversions to your right. Over the next stile; then another; then right, round the edge of the field, and over a small stile ahead into a small copse. Another stile leads into the next field; look straight across to locate the next stile in the beech hedge opposite, which takes you into a green lane.

⑦ Turn right and walk uphill between conifers, on the left, and fields until a metal gate leads on to an open gateway and back on to the airfield.

⑧ Turn left along the edge of the field. Go left over the second iron gate to rejoin the bridleway which leads back to the road. Turn left downhill to find your car.

WHILE YOU'RE THERE

Visit **Broadhembury Craft Centre**, which you will pass as you walk downhill towards the village after Point ④. Open seven days a week and situated in an attractive courtyard setting, here you will find a range of rural craft workshops, as well as the **Corner Café**, serving tea, coffee and light snacks.

Blackborough Whetstone

By contrast – a short extra loop reveals more history.
See map and information panel for Walk 3

•DISTANCE•	2¾ miles (4.4km)
•MINIMUM TIME•	1hr 30min
•ASCENT / GRADIENT•	Negligible
•LEVEL OF DIFFICULTY•	

Walk 4 Directions
(Walk 3 option)

If you feel like a more relaxing alternative, which will teach you something about local industry in the rural heart of Devon, have a look at the nearby village of **Blackborough**. You can always add it to the end of the Broadhembury walk if you want to get a more balanced view of the history of the **Blackdown Hills**.

Leave the car park through the gate opposite the entrance and walk along a broad bridle path, lined with rhododendrons, through Woodland Trust land. This lovely track, with views east over the rolling mid-Devon landscape, leads to a junction of tracks (a little muddy in wet weather). Keep straight on along the bridle path to meet a lane under beech trees. Turn left downhill past pretty cottages to reach **Ponchydown**. Go straight on past the phone box to reach the 'centre' of **Blackborough**. This whole area feels forgotten but a notice board tells you that this remote village was the centre of a flourishing whetstone industry in the 18th and 19th centuries. Whetstones (or 'batts') were used to

sharpen scythes and sickles for cereal harvesting, and were exported to London and even abroad. The locals spoke their own distinct dialect, but the invention of carborundum killed their industry, and by 1900 only three mines remained. This is a fascinating place – ahead you will see old iron gates leading to the wonderfully overgrown churchyard (a haven for wildlife and great for picnics!). The church, which had fallen into disrepair, was demolished in 1994. To the north west lies the Italianate **Blackborough House** (built in 1838), which was never completed, and which has gained a reputation as something of a folly. You can take a slightly different route back to your car by turning right by the notice board and following the footpath sign uphill towards the woods, then almost immediately right again. This leads back to the lane near the bridle path which you follow back to your car.

WHERE TO EAT AND DRINK ⓘ

The **Drewe Arms** in Broadhembury dates from the early Tudor period. It specialises in fish and seafood, has an excellent reputation and a very attractive garden. There is also a café at **Broadhembury Craft Centre,** and, when the gliding club is open, the caterer is happy to serve non-members.

Walk 5

Sidmouth – A Classic Regency Seaside Town

Down the River Sid into Sidmouth in time to take afternoon tea at Connaught Gardens.

•DISTANCE•	3¾ miles (6km)
•MINIMUM TIME•	1hr 30min
•ASCENT / GRADIENT•	Negligible
•LEVEL OF DIFFICULTY•	
•PATHS•	Good level paths or pavements
•LANDSCAPE•	Meadows, town park and seafront
•SUGGESTED MAP•	aqua3 OS Explorer 115 Exeter & Sidmouth
•START / FINISH•	Grid reference: SY 137891
•DOG FRIENDLINESS•	The only thing to look out for is other dogs, of which there will be plenty!
•PARKING•	On roadside near phone box at Fortescue
•PUBLIC TOILETS•	Sidmouth seafront, also at Connaught Gardens

Walk 5 Directions

Originally a small market and fishing town, **Sidmouth** became a popular holiday venue in the late 18th century due to its pleasant scenery and mild climate. With the growth of Torquay in the mid-19th century the rate of Sidmouth's development decreased, so that much of the Georgian architecture remains, unaffected by later Victorian building work.

> **WHILE YOU'RE THERE** ⓘ
> Sidmouth has its own (if smaller) version of the London Planetarium. The **Norman Lockyer Observatory** on Sidmouth Hill, which rises to the east of the town, was founded by Sir Norman Lockyer as an astrophysical research centre in 1912. Since the 1980s it has been run on a voluntary basis. You can go there to learn more about the solar system, carry out your own research, or simply watch the stars – on a clear night, of course.

Considering the civilised nature of the town, it seems fitting that this walk should provide a peaceful, gentle way in. The alternative on foot is along the coast path, which is pretty hard work – the cliffs here rise to over 500ft (150m)!

From Sidford on the A3052 follow signs for **Sidmouth** and **Fortescue**. After a few minutes park safely on the broad road near the phone box on the left. A footpath sign ahead directs you right, down a path to a kissing gate into the grassy meadows by the Sid. Cross the river via a wooden footbridge, then turn left. The path veers away from the river, passes through a kissing gate, and along the field edge to a cross-roads of footpaths. Go left to pass a beautiful wildflower meadow on the left. This is **Gilchrist Field Nature Reserve**, owned and managed by the Sid Vale Association, who aim 'to protect the natural history and wildlife of the area'.

Follow the path on to rejoin the river by a small weir. Just past some pretty cottages (right) cross the wooden footbridge over the river and turn right to enter **The Byes**, parkland with splendid mature trees – lime, holm oak, sweet chestnut, sycamore, willow, copper beech – ideal for a Sunday afternoon stroll to feed the ducks. Keep straight on, passing two footbridges. Just after the next weir leave The Byes through a white metal gate to meet the road by **The Byes Toll House**, built in early 19th-century Greek revival style. The original toll house controlled the eastern approach to the town. Cross over and down **Millford Road**, over the river via a wooden footbridge at a ford, and down **Mill Street**. Turn first left (**Riverside Road**); when that turns sharp right keep straight on past the children's playground to the seafront. There's an invigorating, salty air here – you can buy fresh local seafood – and glorious views.

Turn right to walk along Sidmouth's seafront past delightful Regency terraces, bedecked with hanging baskets in summer. There's a tourist information centre behind the **Port Royal** (Sidmouth Sailing and Sea Angling Club). The long banks of 'boulders' rising from the sea here are part of Sidmouth's sea defences, constructed in the early 1990s to prevent further storm erosion. Pass the **Bedford Hotel**, on the right, and carry on to the end of the promenade. Follow signs for **Connaught Gardens** along the narrow **Clifton Walkway** at the back of the beach. **Note:** Don't walk

here in heavy sea conditions; leave the seafront and continue left uphill away from the town to reach Connaught Gardens (left). The walkway leads under the edge of the marl cliff to overlook the beach at **Jacob's Ladder**, with lovely views to **Peak Hill**.

> **WHERE TO EAT AND DRINK** ⓘ
>
> Sidmouth is bursting with a great range of pubs, cafés and takeaways. The **Bedford Hotel**, situated towards the end of the promenade, has a welcoming atmosphere, good food and an enviable position. The bar overlooks the sea and the views are terrific at all times of year – and in all types of weather. If you're feeling thirsty when you reach Connaught Gardens you can stop for tea in floral surroundings at the licensed **Clocktower Tearooms** (open 364 days of the year, 10AM–5PM). There's also a refreshment kiosk at **Jacob's Ladder beach**.

Turn round and almost immediately climb the metal-railed and very steep steps left up the cliff. Turn left up more steps into **Connaught Gardens** under an arch. Originally part of a private estate, these gardens are a delight all year round, and have won many floral awards. Here too are the **Clocktower Tearooms**. Walk through the gardens away from the sea to the road, turning right downhill to rejoin the promenade. Wander back along the seafront, left up the river, over the footbridge at the ford, and back into **The Byes**. For a change of scene cross the first footbridge and walk up the left bank of the Sid. Go straight past the bridge on which you originally crossed the river and retrace your steps to your car.

Walk 6

Over the Border to Somerset

A long walk from Culmstock to the Wellington Monument.

•DISTANCE•	8 miles (12.9km)
•MINIMUM TIME•	3hrs 30min
•ASCENT / GRADIENT•	590ft (180m) ▲▲▲
•LEVEL OF DIFFICULTY•	🚶 🚶 🚶
•PATHS•	Rough pasture, green lanes and woodland tracks, 16 stiles
•LANDSCAPE•	Rolling farmland and heathery ridge on Blackdown Hills
•SUGGESTED MAP•	aqua3 OS Explorer 128 Taunton & Blackdown Hills
•START / FINISH•	Grid reference: ST 103136
•DOG FRIENDLINESS•	Possibility of livestock in some fields
•PARKING•	Fore Street, Culmstock, near entrance to All Saints Church
•PUBLIC TOILETS•	None on route

BACKGROUND TO THE WALK

One of the landmarks that heralds your approach to Devon as you travel south on the M5 is the Wellington Monument, a strange, triangular obelisk standing 175ft (53.8m) high on the edge of the Blackdown Hills, and particularly impressive when illuminated at night. It's also a great focus for this walk, which starts off through the water-meadows at Culmstock, a quiet village in the Culm valley to the south. Once a small market town with a considerable woollen industry, today it lies off the main tourist trail among rolling fields and peaceful beech woods, a couple of miles from the Somerset border. Several farms, such as beautiful Culm Pyne Barton (passed at Point ⑧), were recorded in the Domesday Book.

Local Hero
The extravagant Wellington monument was erected by local gentry to celebrate the Duke of Wellington's victory at Waterloo in 1815. Earlier military success brought Arthur Wellesley the right to a title: since his family originated from Somerset, he chose the place most closely resembling the family name. He only visited the estate once, in 1819, but local pride was such that his triumphs were publicly celebrated – and in a big way! The foundation stone of the obelisk, on the highest point of the Blackdown Hills (on the Duke's own land), was laid in 1817, but work was not completed until 1892. The trustees gave the estate to the National Trust in 1933. The AA distance board here shows how far you can see in all directions. Amazingly on a clear day you can pick out the Black Mountains in South Wales, 70 miles (113km) north. If you're feeling adventurous (and have a good head for heights) you can borrow the key – and a torch – for a fee from West Monument Farm, just down the road.

Prominent at the start and finish of the walk is All Saints Church. There was a church here in Anglo-Saxon times, but the present building dates from the 14th century. Beautifully light and airy, it's constructed of local flint, the characteristic pinkish colour of Blackdown chert. The tower is adorned by two ferocious gargoyles and four pinnacles, each topped with a weathervane, erected when the original spire was taken down in 1776. Culmstock's famous yew tree, seen on top of the tower, probably took root at that time – it now has a 46cm (18in) trunk and, during the drought of 1976, was painstakingly watered by volunteers; perhaps another example of the pride of these Devon/Somerset borderers.

Walk **6**

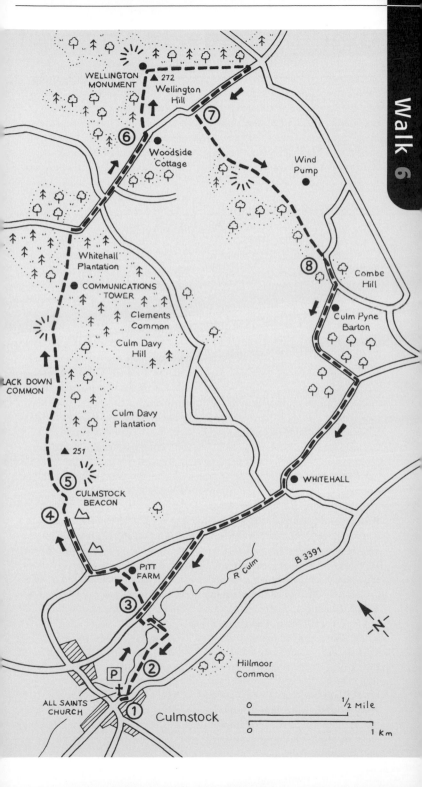

WELLINGTON
MONUMENT

▲ 272
Wellington
Hill

⑦

Wind
Pump

⑥

Woodside
Cottage

Whitehall
Plantation

COMMUNICATIONS
TOWER

⑧

Combe
Hill

Clements
Common

● Culm Pyne
Barton

Culm Davy
Hill

LACK DOWN
COMMON

Culm Davy
Plantation

▲ 251

⑤

CULMSTOCK
BEACON

WHITEHALL

④

③

PITT
FARM

R Culm

B 3391

①

②

ALL SAINTS
CHURCH

Hillmoor
Common

Culmstock

N

0   ½ Mile

0   1 Km

Walk 6

Walk 6 Directions

① Walk along **Fore Street** with the church to the left. As it bends right, take the small lane ahead around the church wall. At 'Cobblestones' turn right towards a kissing gate. Make for the bottom left corner of the field. Go down wooden steps to the river, but don't cross.

② Turn right through a kissing gate towards a stile below two ash trees. A wooden footbridge takes you across the river. Turn left, then right and over a stile in the hedge. Head over the next stile towards stables, and on to a lane. Turn right.

WHAT TO LOOK FOR   ⓘ

Ascent of the steep, flinty, muddy path to the vantage point of **Culmstock Beacon** on the edge of Blackdown Common is rewarded by fantastic views. This restored beacon hut was part of the network of beacons set up across England to provide an early warning system at the time of the Spanish Armada in the summer of 1588. The one at Culmstock linked with others at North Upottery, Holcombe Regis and Blackborough.

---

③ Just past the cream-coloured house (right), turn left through a wooden gate. Walk straight up the field with the hedge on your left. When the hedge veers left aim for the top right corner of the field and a stile, crossing it to continue uphill across the field. Through a gate, follow the track left of **Pitt Farm**. where a gate leads to the farm drive. Turn left; then, where the drive meets a lane, turn right uphill.

④ The lane becomes a rough track and turns left; a few steps round the corner turn right through a small gate and climb up to the trig point on **Culmstock Beacon**.

⑤ Pass to the right of the trig point and follow the ridge on a level flinty track. Keep out in the open here and aim for the communications tower ahead to your right. Cut right towards the mast from a broad grassy ride, through a metal gate into beech woods, and take the broad track ahead. The path eventually leaves the trees and runs downhill to join a tarmac road; carry straight on to meet a larger road on a sharp bend, and continue straight ahead.

⑥ When the road curves right turn left over a stile and up the field; over two stiles, then a third in the top corner to the monument. Turn right down the approach track to meet the road and turn right again.

⑦ Just before the road bends right take the footpath signed left over a stile. Cross the field and the next stile onto a little-used grassy path. Cross the next two stiles and the field to enter a beech wood by a stile. Emerging from the woodland by another stile, carry straight on and over two more stiles to meet the lane. Turn right.

⑧ After 250yds (229m) turn right downhill, then right at the first junction. Go straight ahead through the hamlet of **Whitehall** and follow the lane to the house at Point ③. Turn left past the house and retrace your steps home.

WHERE TO EAT AND DRINK   ⓘ

There are two pubs in Culmstock. The **Ilminster Stage**, opposite the church, is a free house with a courtyard and beer garden. The **Culm Valley Inn** (free house) is by the River Culm, and has benches and tables in an attractive setting by the river. Both serve a good range of bar food and welcome children.

Bickleigh Castle and the Exe Valley Way

Leave the crowds behind at Bickleigh Bridge and explore the lovely Exe Valley.

Walk 7

•DISTANCE•	4 miles (6.4km)
•MINIMUM TIME•	2hrs
•ASCENT / GRADIENT•	509ft (155m) ▲▲▲
•LEVEL OF DIFFICULTY•	🚶 🚶 🚶
•PATHS•	Country lanes, one long, steep, muddy track
•LANDSCAPE•	Steeply wooded hillsides and farmland
•SUGGESTED MAP•	aqua3 OS Explorer 114 Exeter & the Exe Valley
•START / FINISH•	Grid reference: SX 939075
•DOG FRIENDLINESS•	Can run free on lanes and tracks
•PARKING•	Bickleigh Mill just off A396 at Bickleigh Bridge
•PUBLIC TOILETS•	Trout Inn – available to public during opening hours

BACKGROUND TO THE WALK

The honeypot area round Bickleigh Bridge, 4 miles (6.4km) south of Tiverton, may be too crowded for many people, and I, for one, am always tempted to drive straight through to escape the mass of visitors and cars. But dozens of people do stop here to take a picture of the Bickleigh Cottage Country Hotel, the picturesque thatched building just above the bridge, instantly recognisable from many 'Beautiful Britain' calendars, and which must be one of the most photographed scenes in Devon. But if it's all too much for you there is a quieter side to this part of the Exe Valley, and within a few minutes' walk from the bridge you will feel as if you are miles from anywhere.

Family Outing

Bickleigh Mill, at the beginning of the walk, is a good place to entertain the family, with craft, gift and workshops, and a working mill. There's a children's pet area, and the Devon Railway Centre, centred on the Victorian Great Western Railway station, with train rides and model railways. Footpaths lead us to the unspoilt village of Bickleigh, with pretty thatched cottages, the 14th-century church of St Mary the Virgin and a graceful Regency vicarage.

Mixed Up Castle

Bickleigh Castle is in a peaceful backwater on the banks of the River Exe. The walk approaches it along a quiet lane, shaded by huge oak, ash and beech trees. An interesting mixture of Norman, medieval and 17th-century architecture, it's a thatched, moated manor house, rather than a castle, and is still lived in. It passed to the de Bickleigh family after the Norman Conquest and was recorded in the Domesday Book. The chapel was built in the 11th century. In the 15th century it belonged to the Courtenays, Earls of Devon, and later to the Carews. Much of the castle was destroyed during the Civil War, and rebuilt in a more homely style. The pink sandstone three-storey gatehouse and moated garden, visible from the lane, are both quite beautiful. There are limited opening hours (the castle is never open on Saturdays) – but it's worth finding out when you can have a proper look round.

Walk 7

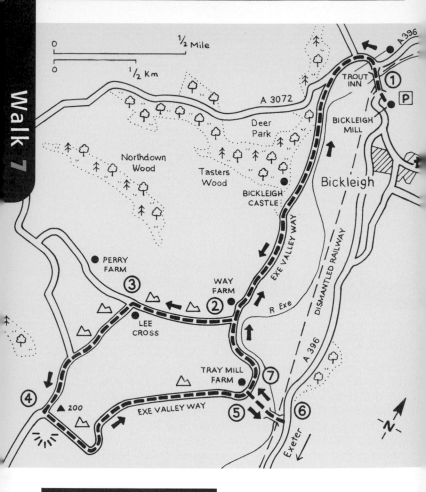

Walk 7 Directions

① From the public parking area at the edge of **Bickleigh Mill** go back, with care, to the A396 and cross the bridge. Turn left down the A3072, following the brown tourist sign for **Bickleigh Castle**. Take the first lane left, running along the edge of the flood plain on the **Exe Valley Way** (EVW). Bickleigh Castle will soon be found on the right. Go straight on past **Way Farm**.

② Just after the buildings of **Way Farm** turn right to leave the **Exe Valley Way**, roughly signposted

'**Lee Cross & Perry Farm**'. This deeply banked, ancient lane climbs steeply uphill and after 700yds (640m) brings you to the farm at **Lee Cross**.

> ### WHILE YOU'RE THERE ⓘ
> Visit **Yearlstone Vineyard**, signposted left off the A396 just north of Bickleigh Bridge. The vineyard is the oldest in Devon, and one of the best in the South West. Situated on a steep, south-facing slope above the confluence of the River Exe and the smaller River Dart, it commands views over Bickleigh and the Exe Valley. The vineyard is open for visitors from 11AM to 5PM from Friday to Monday, April to October.

Walk 7

③ Immediately after the house and stables turn left up a green lane, climbing steadily to pass a ruined brick-built chapel over the hedge right, just beyond which another green lane joins from the right. Go straight on; the lane levels off and becomes easier.

> ### WHERE TO EAT AND DRINK
> The **Fisherman's Cot** lies just below Bickleigh Bridge, and has an attractive riverside garden, from which you get a really good view of the beautiful 16th-century five-arched bridge over the Exe. It's not a particularly cosy or personal pub, but can cater for large numbers at any time. The 17th-century **Trout Inn**, just a little upriver, also provides good food and welcomes families. There is a licensed café/bar and restaurant at Bickleigh Mill.

④ Where the green lane meets the tarmac lane turn left and proceed steeply downhill (EVW). The views over the **River Exe**, and to **Silverton church** beyond, are glorious. Follow the lane down until you see **Tray Mill Farm** on the right.

> ### WHAT TO LOOK FOR
> Watch the **salmon** leaping up the weir just below the bridge. This stretch of the Exe is very popular with game fishermen, but the fishing rights are privately owned. Salmon and sea trout fishing licences are available from the Environment Agency, and the season on the Exe runs from mid-February to the end of September. There are strict conservation measures in force to protect spring salmon. The record on the Exe is a fish of over 30lbs (13.6kg) in weight, caught by a man who had never fished for salmon before!

⑤ The way home is straight on along the lane, but it's worth doing a small detour to the river here. Turn right through the farmyard (no sign) and pass through a metal gate onto a concrete standing. Ahead you will see a suspension bridge over the river; cross it and go straight on to reach the dismantled railway track. Do not turn left along the track – although it would take you straight back to your car– it is privately owned and has no public right of way.

⑥ The path goes straight on here to meet the A369. You can do that, turn left, then eventually right to walk through **Bickleigh** village back to the mill, but it is a busy road and you would be better advised to retrace your steps to **Tray Mill Farm** and take the quieter route back to **Bickleigh Mill**.

⑦ Back on the lane by **Tray Mill Farm**, turn right and walk straight along the lane, past **Bickleigh Castle**, turning right at the A3072, and right again over the bridge to return to your car.

Walk 8

The Birdlife of the Otter Estuary Nature Reserve

Along the banks of the peaceful River Otter and the red sandstone cliffs towards High Peak.

•DISTANCE•	4¼ miles (7km)
•MINIMUM TIME•	2hrs
•ASCENT / GRADIENT•	164ft (50m)
•LEVEL OF DIFFICULTY•	
•PATHS•	Good level paths, coastal section and lanes, 2 stiles
•LANDSCAPE•	River meadow, cliffs and undulating farmland
•SUGGESTED MAP•	aqua3 OS Explorer 115 Exeter & Sidmouth
•START / FINISH•	Grid reference: SX 077830
•DOG FRIENDLINESS•	Opportunities for dogs to run free; some livestock
•PARKING•	By side of broad, quiet lane near entrance to South Farm
•PUBLIC TOILETS•	None on main route. Otterton Mill on Walk 9

BACKGROUND TO THE WALK

Peaceful, tranquil, lush, idyllic – these are all words that could easily be applied to this stroll along the banks of the River Otter. The river wends its way to meet the sea just east of Budleigh Salterton, its lower reaches a haven for a wealth of birdlife. In contrast to this, the walk continues along the top of the red sandstone cliffs typical of this area – but the coast path here is not in any way heart-thumpingly strenuous. The combination of the serene river meadows and the glorious coastal scenery – and then, perhaps, tea at Otterton Mill – make this an ideal family walk.

The Otter Estuary Nature Reserve

The Nature Reserve, south of White Bridge and managed by the Devon Wildlife Trust, is one of the smallest in the South West. The estuary was much more extensive in the past, and 500 years ago cargo ships could travel upriver as far as Otterton. Today the estuary provides a haven for all kinds of birdlife, best seen between October and March. Oystercatchers, dunlins and other wading birds come to feed here; large flocks of waders and ducks, such as wigeons and teal, attract peregrine falcons, sparrowhawks and mink. There are over 200,000 wigeon on British estuaries, and it is one of our most common over-wintering species of duck. Three-quarters of the estuary has been colonised by saltmarsh, which is also home to warblers in the summer months, linnets and greenfinches all year round, and kingfishers in winter. To catch the action, about ¼ mile (400m) from the start of the main walk take a small path right towards the river to a birdwatching hide, run by the Devon Birdwatching and Preservation Society. Stop for a while and watch the activity on the waters below – there's always something happening.

The mid-section of the walk brings us within sight of Otterton, a large, pleasant village, with many traditional cob and thatch buildings. The church – St Michael and All Angels – is most impressive. There was a Saxon church here before the Norman Conquest, rebuilt by Benedictine monks when they established a priory in the 12th century. The main monastery building lay on the north side of the church, and part of it – probably the guests' hall – remains today. After Henry VIII's Dissolution of the Monasteries, in 1539, the church gradually fell into disrepair until it was, eventually, totally rebuilt in the 1870s. The design was by Benjamin Ferrey and the funding came from the Rt Hon Louisa Lady Rolle, a local dignitary. The church today is extremely grand and spacious, with superb blue marble columns along the nave. The west tower is built of the Old Red Sandstone we saw in the cliffs earlier in the walk.

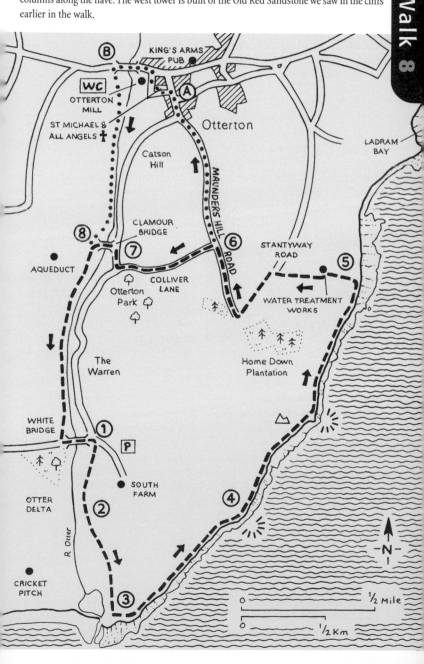

Walk 8

Walk 8 Directions

① Walk through the kissing gate to the right of the gate to **South Farm**. Turn right following signs for '**Coast Path Ladram Bay**'. The narrow, sandy path runs along the field edge, with lovely views right over the saltmarshes of the **Otter Estuary Nature Reserve** and the **River Otter**.

② At the end of that field a shallow flight of wooden steps leads to a walkway and footbridge, and up into the next field. There are good views downriver to the shingle bank at **Budleigh Salterton** and across the river to the cricket pitch.

WHILE YOU'RE THERE ⓘ
Visit **Bicton Park** and **Botanical Gardens**, straight over the B3178 from the road to Otterton. Bicton is open 364 days of the year, and has over 60 acres (24ha) of landscaped gardens, with a superb arboretum, lake and a secret garden, and a splendid 19th-century Palm House.

③ The path continues gently downhill until it turns sharply left following the line of the coast. Just before you turn east there are panoramic views right over the Otter delta, and along the beach.

④ After just over a mile (1.6km) the path rises a little, and you can see the whole of **Lyme Bay** ahead, including **High Peak** (564ft/157m – one of the highest points on the South Devon coast). Follow the coast path: the red sandstone cliffs are extremely friable and 'chunks' continually tumble seawards, but the path is safe. Pass through a small gate by the ruined lookout building, and downhill.

⑤ Turn left to leave the coast path on the '**Permissive path to Otterton**'; this narrow, grassy path leads over a stile; turn immediately left and follow the path right around the water treatment works, and up the gravelly lane to meet **Stantyway Road**. The lane veers right, but you should turn left up a grassy track, following signs to **Otterton** and the **River Otter**. The track soon veers right and gives way to a tarmac lane.

⑥ After 400yds (366m) **Colliver Lane** and the **River Otter** are signed to the left. Turn left here and follow a narrow, wooded green lane, which ends at a gate. Go through that, then almost immediately another, and follow the signs along the edge of the next field, which you leave over a stile onto a track.

⑦ Turn immediately left between two big ornamental brick pillars, and then right under a very large oak tree. Descend a short flight of steps and cross over the River **Otter** on **Clamour Bridge**, a wooden footbridge.

⑧ Turn left and follow the river south; over a small leat (look out for the aqueduct coming across the meadows on your right), through a gate and continue to **White Bridge**, where you go through a kissing gate, turn left and find your car.

WHERE TO EAT AND DRINK ⓘ
If you just do the main walk, drive up to the village of Otterton afterwards. The café at **Otterton Mill** is open daily from 10AM to 5PM (early closing in winter) and serves a great range of delicious wholefood dishes. The **King's Arms** (complete with its own post office) welcomes families, and has a beer garden and children's play area.

A Trip to Otterton Mill

A beautiful church – and one of the last working mills in the county.
See map and information panel for Walk 8

•DISTANCE•	5½ miles (9km)
•MINIMUM TIME•	2hrs 30min
•ASCENT / GRADIENT•	189ft (58m) ▲▲▲
•LEVEL OF DIFFICULTY•	🚶🚶 🚶🚶 🚶🚶

Walk 9 Directions (Walk 8 option)

You can easily extend Walk 8 by adding on a loop which will take you to **Otterton Mill** in Otterton village; both are worth a visit.

Leave the main route at Point ⑥; go straight on up the tarmac lane, following the Public Right of Way signs along **Maunders Hill Road**. This pretty lane climbs gently up before dropping down to reach the edge of **Otterton** village. Turn left at Point Ⓐ along **Green Close**, and through the lychgate into the churchyard of **St Michaels & All Angels** (➤ Walk 8, Background); it's most impressive and well worth a look. Leave the church via its main door and go down **Church Hill** to join the road through the village. Turn left for **Otterton Mill**. The **King's Arms** pub will be found a few paces to the right on the opposite side of the road. Otterton Mill has been in operation for 1,000 years, and is the last working mill on the **River Otter** – and one of the last remaining working watermills in the county. It's a great place for a break. There are craft workshops,

a museum and gallery, and an exhibition of East Devon lace, an important cottage industry in the area for over 400 years. You can enjoy a snack at the **Duckery Restaurant**, and buy some of the best stoneground bread in Devon from the **Barn Bakery**. To continue the walk go past the mill and over the bridge, then immediately left at Point Ⓑ to walk along the riverbank. The **River Otter** is slow and broad here, with beautiful willows and beech trees lining the opposite bank. Just over ½ mile (800m) from the mill you reach the **Clamour Bridge** through a cantilevered gate, to rejoin the main route at Point ⑦.

WHAT TO LOOK FOR ⓘ

The smallest of the grebe family, the **little grebe**, although rare in Devon, has been spotted near White Bridge. Naturally clumsy on land, all members of the grebe family become experts when they hit the water. The little grebe (about 10–12in (25–30cm) long), often called the 'dabchick', is a busy little bird, diving and bobbing up again in its search for food. When it becomes alarmed it will submerge its whole body under the water. It has a distinctive chestnut throat and a pale patch near the base of the bill, and flies low over the water with a rapid, whirring action.

Walk 10

The Grand Western Canal Country Park

A wealth of wildlife – and an important piece of industrial archaeology.

•DISTANCE•	5 miles (8km)
•MINIMUM TIME•	2hrs
•ASCENT / GRADIENT•	Negligible
•LEVEL OF DIFFICULTY•	
•PATHS•	Canal tow path
•LANDSCAPE•	Mixed farmland, canal-side on edge of Tiverton
•SUGGESTED MAP•	aqua3 OS Explorer 114 Exeter & the Exe Valley
•START / FINISH•	Grid reference: SX 998131
•DOG FRIENDLINESS•	Keep dogs under control while in country park
•PARKING•	Parking and picnic area at Tiverton Road Bridge
•PUBLIC TOILETS•	Grand Western Canal Basin

Walk 10 Directions

Just a few miles west of Junction 27 on the busy M5 lies another world. The **Grand Western Canal**, built between 1810 and 1814 and never completed, provides the opportunity for a really lovely, easy afternoon stroll just to the east of **Tiverton.** Now run as a country park, the reed-fringed tow path along this stretch of canal (the whole being just over 11 miles/ 18km long) invites you to walk to the canal basin in Tiverton.

The original plan, formulated by James Brindley in 1768, was for a canal system that would link Bristol to Exeter. In 1796 an Act of Parliament was obtained for the building of the Grand Western Canal, to run from Topsham (south of Exeter) to Taunton, with three branches – to Cullompton, Tiverton and Wellington. But due to the Napoleonic Wars the scheme was dropped until 1810, when the route

was re-surveyed by John Rennie, and work began. The section from Lowdwells to Tiverton opened in 1814, at a cost of over £220,000. The section from Taunton to Lowdwells opened in 1838, but was never profitable and closed in 1869. The development of the railway system in the area in the mid-19th century heralded an end to the commercial use of the canal, which became used primarily by barges

WHERE TO EAT AND DRINK

The **Canal Tea Room & Gardens,** a listed 16th-century cottage (now the only one in Tiverton) and pretty garden (complete with water features), is situated to the right of the canal basin as you approach it on this walk. Open every day from 10AM to 6PM it is licensed, the food is excellent, and you can be assured of a warm welcome. Ice creams are also sold here. Refreshments are available at the canal basin itself; there is an **information kiosk,** also selling gifts, and a barge – **'Teas Afloat'** – moored in the basin. The **Barge Inn** can be found on the A361 at Holbeton towards Sampford Peverell.

conveying limestone from the quarries at Westleigh. These travelled to the Tiverton Basin where the limestone was processed in lime kilns, which can still be seen today, to be transported away by road. Operations only finally stopped in 1924. Wharves and lime kilns can also be seen south of Waytown Tunnel at Lowdwells to the north.

There are plenty of parking spaces at the **Tiverton Road Bridge**, and an attractive picnic area in the bend of the canal, on the site of one of the wharves where stone was unloaded and crushed for use in road-making. Park here and walk over the sandstone bridge, then left to join the canal. Turn left under the bridge (the canal will be to your right). Many of the bridges display mason's marks, and there are some here: the stonemasons marked their work so that poor work could be traced to the right culprit!

This section of the canal and tow path is extremely pretty. The water is edged with a broad band of white waterlilies, and you will see coots, moorhens and mallards. Typical flowers include hemp agrimony, arrowhead, cuckoo flower and yellow iris. As you leave the road behind you are likely to see a heron and, if you're lucky, a kingfisher.

Cross the canal at **Crownhill** (or Change Path) **Bridge**, where there's another picnic area. Turn left and continue along the tow path. The canal runs over an aqueduct, built in 1847, 40ft (12m) above the now dismantled Tiverton-to-Tiverton Junction line. Just past the aqueduct there are glorious views left across farmland towards the **Blackdown Hills**. The path continues to **East**

Manley Bridge, **Manley Bridge** and **Warnicombe Bridge**, where there are glorious willows, oak, ash and beech trees. You may well see a brightly painted horse-drawn barge here; the Grand Western Horseboat Company operates trips along the canal from March to December.

There is a milestone just before the next bridge, **Tidcombe Bridge**, though its inscription is now indecipherable. As the edge of Tiverton is reached, neat gardens front the water's edge. The tow path passes under a modern footbridge, then an old stone bridge pier on the opposite bank, still showing the grooves for a stop-gate. This would have been used to seal off part of the canal in times of emergency or when repairs were needed to this section. The canal basin is reached after 2½ miles (4km) of pleasant, gentle walking – and it's pretty easy to find your way home!

Walk 11

The National Trust at Killerton

A gentle parkland and woodland walk around the National Trust's beautiful Killerton Estate.

•DISTANCE•	4¼ miles (7km)
•MINIMUM TIME•	2hrs 15min
•ASCENT / GRADIENT•	131ft (40m) ▲▲ ▲
•LEVEL OF DIFFICULTY•	🚶🚶 🚶🚶 🚶🚶
•PATHS•	Good footpaths, bridleways and farm tracks, 3 stiles
•LANDSCAPE•	Gently undulating woodland and parkland
•SUGGESTED MAP•	aqua3 OS Explorer 114 Exeter & the Exe Valley
•START / FINISH•	Grid reference: SX 977001
•DOG FRIENDLINESS•	Keep on lead in park
•PARKING•	National Trust car park plus overflow car park
•PUBLIC TOILETS•	Between car park and stable courtyard

BACKGROUND TO THE WALK

This gentle exploration of the countryside around the National Trust estate at Killerton, just north of Exeter and given to the Trust by Sir Richard Acland in 1944, uses a variety of well-maintained public footpaths and bridleways, but doesn't actually enter the grounds (for which a fee is charged). Killerton estate was formed by the Acland family. Their original house (of which only the gatehouse and chapel remain) was at Columbjohn, and was used by the King's troops during the siege of Exeter in the Civil War. Killerton is well worth a visit: quite apart from the house, rebuilt in 1778 to the design of John Johnson, and delightful gardens (with colour-coded waymarked walks) there is a National Trust shop, tea room and plant centre in the old stable block and courtyard. The whole estate comprises 6,400 acres (2,591ha) and includes Ashclyst Forest, 2 miles (3.2km) to the east (with waymarked walks), the Red Lion pub in the village of Broadclyst, to the south, and the paper mill by Ellerhayes Bridge.

A Glorious Setting

The park and gardens at Killerton were created in the late 18th century, making full use of the contours of the natural landscape, and are characterised by a wide variety of exotic tree species, including tall Wellingtonias (named after the Duke of Wellington). The storms of January 1990 caused considerable damage, and have been followed by a programme of intensive replanting. The gardens feature magnolias, azaleas and rhododendrons on the wooded slopes above the house, and superb herbaceous borders on the lower levels. As you enter the parkland at Point ② you pass some splendid examples of cedar of Lebanon and holm oak, and a beautiful weeping willow on an island in a pond (left). Just past the house the walk leads uphill near the memorial to Sir Thomas Dyke Acland, and you can enjoy good views west towards the Exe Valley and beyond to Cosdon Hill on Dartmoor. Gilbert Davis, the longest serving gardener at any National Trust property in Devon, finally retired from his duties here in November 2000, after a staggering 50 years.

Beware Dragons…

In Columbjohn Wood badger tracks abound, and in spring the air is heavy with the scent of wild garlic. You may glimpse roe deer, or even a fox; you will certainly hear the deep croak of ravens, and the mewing cry of a buzzard soaring overhead. But look out for the dragon which travels by underground tunnel between the twin Iron Age hillforts of Dolbury Hill, which lies just north of the house in the centre of the estate (not visited) and Cadbury Castle, 6 miles (9.7km) to the north west!

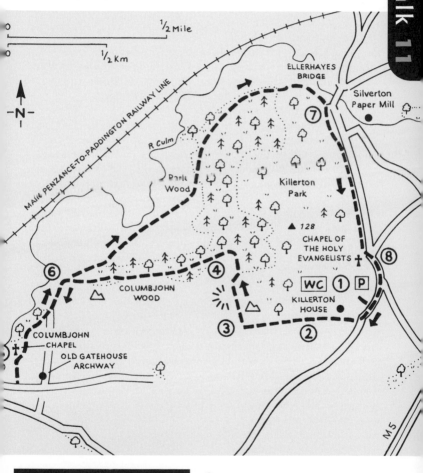

Walk 11 Directions

① From the car park return to the road and turn right to reach the gate and cattle grid at the entrance drive to **Killerton House**. Follow the public footpath sign towards the house, passing the stables and courtyard on the right from where ticket holders approach the house.

② You have to leave this main approach drive as it gets closer to Killerton House itself. You will pass the house on your right-hand side. Continue straight on, past the estate's walled gardens and ornamental lawns. Shortly after, cross a stile on the right and continue through the small gate in the hedge ahead. This takes you into a large sloping field.

Walk 11

③ Turn right uphill, keeping by the hedge and then metal fence on your right. At the top of the field ignore the public footpath sign '**Bluebell Gate**', and turn left down across the field to go enter **Columbjohn Wood** through a small gate marked 'Beware of walkers'.

④ Take the bridle path left, and immediately branch left again on the higher path, which leads gradually downhill. Leave the wood by another gate, and keep straight on to meet and follow a farm track. After 250yds (229m) cross the stile on the right to enter a field. Keeping the wood on your right pass a cottage to arrive at the peaceful 16th-century **Columbjohn Chapel**.

> **WHERE TO EAT AND DRINK** ⓘ
> There is a licensed restaurant and tea room at **Killerton House**, and a good pub – the **Red Lion** – attractively situated by the church in Broadclyst, 2½ miles (4km) south on the B3181.

⑤ Cross another stile to gain the grassy drive opposite the chapel, and take a look at the old gatehouse archway. Retrace your steps through the field back to the farm track.

⑥ Turn left and follow this delightful level track through woods and fields around the edge of the estate. The **River Culm** can be seen on your left, but you will

> **WHAT TO LOOK FOR** ⓘ
> **Columbjohn Chapel** burial ground is dominated by the graves of the Acland family; look out for the tombstone of the Silverton stationmaster. Unfortunately the chapel is used as a storeroom and kept locked, but the stone doorway and simple bell tower are quite charming. It's an ideal spot to pause for a while and enjoy a quiet moment of reflection.

> **WHILE YOU'RE THERE** ⓘ
> Go and have a look at **Killerton** itself, which is open from mid-March to late October (National Trust members free). The house contains the Paulise de Bush costume collection and a Victorian laundry, and in the gardens you can find an ice house and the Bear's Hut, an early 19th-century summerhouse.

be more aware of the main Penzance-to-Paddington railway. The track reaches the road by **Ellerhayes Bridge**.

⑦ Do not go onto the road; turn right to follow the edge of the undulating parkland and woods, keeping the road on your left. You will pass through several gates marked '**National Trust bridlepath**' to eventually join a gravel track which passes the entrance to the **Chapel of the Holy Evangelists**, built in the Norman style in 1842 for the Aclands, their tenants and employees, and to replace the one at Columbjohn.

⑧ Continue on to meet the road. Turn right through a cutting, and again branch right, following signs to **Killerton House**, to reach the car park.

The Buzzards Walk

A walk through peaceful hillside woods and riverbanks in mid Devon.

•DISTANCE•	3¾ miles (6km)
•MINIMUM TIME•	2hrs
•ASCENT / GRADIENT•	150ft (45m) ▲▲▲
•LEVEL OF DIFFICULTY•	🚶 🚶 🚶
•PATHS•	Waymarked paths, tracks and quiet lanes, 3 stiles
•LANDSCAPE•	Wooded hillsides and riverbanks
•SUGGESTED MAP•	aqua3 OS Explorer 114 Exeter & the Exe Valley
•START / FINISH•	Grid reference: SX 905121
•DOG FRIENDLINESS•	Dogs should be kept under control, livestock in some fields
•PARKING•	A narrow lane (No Through Road) leads to car park from B3137 near sign to Withleigh church
•PUBLIC TOILETS•	None on route

BACKGROUND TO THE WALK

There are three, little-known but nonetheless wonderful, areas of National Trust woodland – Cross's Wood, Thongsleigh Wood and Huntland Wood – tucked away in the secluded and undulating mid-Devon countryside to the west of Tiverton. This walk, in an area that is very much off the beaten track, explores these lovely woodlands draping over the steep hillsides above the valley of the tiny River Dart, which runs into the River Exe at nearby Bickleigh.

There are several excellent picnic spots along the route, the best one being reached at Point ④ where you can take a break on a high level open area after climbing up through Cross's Wood. It also gives you the opportunity to spend some quality time admiring that magnificent bird of prey so typical of this kind of landscape – the buzzard.

Buzzards

Watching a pair of common buzzards gliding effortlessly through the sky has to be one of the most magnificent sights above the hills and wooded valleys of the West Country. Using updraughts to soar overhead, their broad wings held forward and wing feathers extended, these most common of the larger raptors scan the ground below for their prey – small mammals, and rabbits in particular. Their characteristic 'whee-eur' call is frequently heard in hilly country, and if you're lucky enough to see one perched upright on a fence post you will notice it has a heavily barred tail, a small head and a black, hooked bill. Quite often you will see a lone buzzard being mobbed by crows. With the decline in persecution by gamekeepers, and with a plentiful supply of rabbits available, the buzzard population of the country now runs to tens of thousands.

By contrast the scarce honey buzzard is one of the country's rarest breeders. It lives on a diet of wild bees and their honey, as well as on other insects. This rather refined food source may be supplemented occasionally by small mammals. The honey buzzard is only a summer visitor to southern England, and fewer than a dozen pairs attempt to nest each year. They are very unusual in this part of Devon but have been spotted over the Haldon Hills to the south west of Exeter.

The woods, fields and banks encountered on this walk are full of interest all year round. As well as a glorious range of wild flowers, there is a fantastic babble of birdsong here in spring and summer, and a chance of seeing roe deer, and in the early evening perhaps a badger trundling along the path. You should also see dragonflies skimming over the sparkling waters of the Dart. The walk follows waymarked paths and tracks through the woodland, parts of which can be muddy at any time of year.

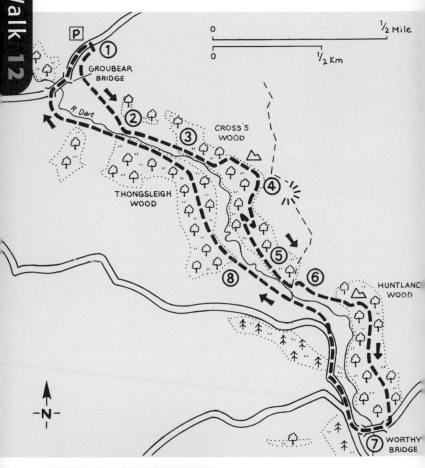

Walk 12 **Directions**

① From the car park cross the stile into a field, and turn right. At the hedge ahead turn left and walk towards the wood. Drop down steeply right, heading for the gate and a stone water trough near by.

② Once through the gate go straight ahead, keeping the hedge

left. Cross the next stile and continue with the tiny **River Dart** on the right. Before the bridge turn left at the waymarker, through a small gate into another field. Turn right, keeping the high hedge right.

③ Leave the field through the next gate, which leads onto a broad track which rises through **Cross's Wood**. Soon after passing a bench a waymarker directs you left, off the

Walk 12

track and back into the woods up a fairly steep, narrow path, a little overgrown and muddy in places. Continue to climb until the path reaches a wide track at the top of the woods.

④ Turn right to follow the track gently downhill, through a gate into an open area where it zig-zags more steeply downhill between gorse, broom and bracken.

WHAT TO LOOK FOR
Deciduous woodlands such as these support a great variety of wild flowers. Shade-loving plants abound, but many early flowers bloom in spring before the leaf canopy shuts out too much light. Ancient woods are very stable plant communities, and some species such as ramsons – wild garlic – are evidence of old, undisturbed woodland. Look out too for primroses in early spring, and delicate wood anemones; then in May the carpet of bluebells so typical of this sort of habitat.

⑤ Continue on to the valley bottom and join the riverside track, passing through a gate with a sign asking horse-riders to dismount. Before the bridge ahead turn left on a broad track. After a few paces turn right over a stile and double-plank bridge to enter a field.

⑥ Keep the high hedge on your left and walk through the field for about 250yds (229m) to reach a small gate into **Huntland Wood**. Follow the path steeply uphill. It levels off and leads through the beautiful upper part of the wood before descending gradually to leave the wood at a lane.

⑦ Turn right and proceed downhill, cross the Dart at **Worthy Bridge**, turn right at the next junction and past some houses.

WHERE TO EAT AND DRINK
There is nothing very close by, but there are two pubs at Pennymoor, 5 miles (8km) further west. The **Cruwys Arms** is not open at lunchtime Monday to Thursday. The **Mount Pleasant** is open all day and serves good food. There's also the **Cadeleigh Arms** at Cadeleigh to the south of the walk, with real ale, excellent food and a pretty garden, but it's a bit of a trek along narrow, winding lanes to get there.

Where the lane bends left, go straight ahead through a gate onto a track, which you follow (with the river to your right) through a gate and into **Thongsleigh Wood**.

⑧ Continue along the track, with the river right. At a small gate leave the wood and enter some meadows; the path here is faint but continues straight ahead. The next gate (rather decrepit) leads onto a lane. Turn right over **Groubear Bridge** and climb back up the ancient rocky lane to the car park.

WHILE YOU'RE THERE
Take a trip to **Knightshayes Court**, signposted off the A396 at Bolham, 2 miles (3.2km) north of Tiverton. The family home of the Heathcoat Amorys, this splendid house looks down on Tiverton and on the site of the lace-making factory set up by industrialist John Heathcoat in 1815, which once employed 1,500 people, and from which the family gained their wealth. The house was begun in 1869 under John Heathcoat's grandson, and designed by William Burges. You really do get an impression of grand 19th-century country house life here. The gardens, which merge into woodland, are superb, especially in spring. There are some fine topiary animals on the box hedges near the house. The National Trust has established an excellent restaurant, shop and plant centre in the old stables.

Walk 13

The Bampton Notts

Stories from a little-known corner of North East Devon.

•DISTANCE•	5½ miles (9km)
•MINIMUM TIME•	2hrs 30min
•ASCENT / GRADIENT•	425ft (130m) ▲▲▲
•LEVEL OF DIFFICULTY•	🚶🚶 🚶🚶 🚶
•PATHS•	Rough fields, tracks and lanes, 11 stiles
•LANDSCAPE•	Rolling hills and wooded combes
•SUGGESTED MAP•	aqua3 OS Explorer 114 Exeter & the Exe Valley
•START / FINISH•	Grid reference: SX 956223
•DOG FRIENDLINESS•	On lead on B3190, livestock in some fields
•PARKING•	Station Road car park by church in centre of Bampton
•PUBLIC TOILETS•	By car park

BACKGROUND TO THE WALK

Bampton is one of those places that isn't really on the way to anywhere. As you drive north towards Exmoor from Tiverton you might sweep past the turning to Bampton, making for Dulverton up the Barle Valley. But it would be a mistake not to go and have a look at this quiet, ancient town, situated at a natural crossing place on the River Batherm, and whose Saxon origins are still evident in the layout of its building plots, streets and almost circular churchyard. In 1258 a royal charter established St Luke's Fair, one of the oldest in the country, which became famous for the October sale of Exmoor ponies in the late 19th century, and which survives today as a funfair and street market. It's an unspoilt town where the tradition of taking your Christmas Day turkey to the bakery to be cooked still carries on.

An Agricultural Community

Bampton held important cattle and wool sheep markets from the 14th century, and the various fine buildings in the town to be seen today are evidence of wealthier times in the 17th and 18th centuries, when the cloth industry was at its most prosperous. The town was famous for the Bampton Notts, said to be the finest breed of sheep in Devon, but which died out in the late 19th century. Before the coming of the railway in 1884 the sheep were herded on foot to Bristol, 60 miles (197km) away, for sale.

It's worth deviating from your route a little to have a look at the church of St Michael and All Angels in Bampton, dating in part from the 12th century, though an earlier one occupied the site. A late Saxon or early Norman window arch can be seen high in the south wall. An interesting feature here is the stone casing around two enormous yew trees in the churchyard, to prevent the sheep that used to graze here from being poisoned. The roots of these huge trees may be responsible for the cracks that have appeared in the south wall.

As the walk penetrates deeper into the Devon countryside, it reaches the tiny village of Morebath, essentially a farming community, as it has been since Saxon times. It has a remote, yet safe, feel about it. There are warm springs of chalybeate water here in a marshy basin, from which the name Morebath derives. The simple tower of St George's Church probably dates from the 11th century but its most unusual feature is the saddleback roof, part of the 19th-century restoration, which is unlike anything seen elsewhere in the county.

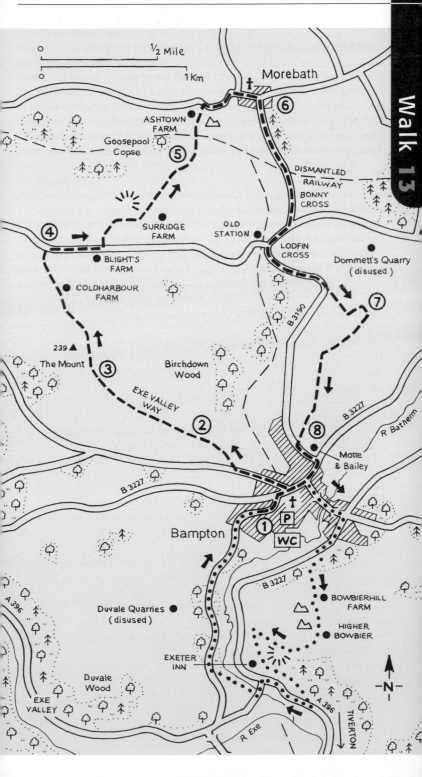

Walk 13

Walk 13 Directions

① Leave the car park by the toilets, cross the road and turn left up the steep, narrow lane signposted '**Dulverton**'. After a few minutes follow **Exe Valley Way** (EVW) signs right up a drive, left through a gate and up the field keeping right. Cross over the stile and go left on the track to reach a double stile in the top corner of the field. Over that, turn immediately right over another then turn left through a bank of trees and right, uphill (keeping the trees right).

② Follow EVW signs over the next stile, straight across the field to another stile (top left) and left around the field to an open gateway. Turn left, then immediately right, keeping the hedge on your left to reach a metal gate at the hilltop, with views towards Exmoor.

> **WHERE TO EAT AND DRINK** ⓘ
> Try the characterful 200-year-old **Seahorse**, a real ale pub on Briton Street at the other end of the town from the car park. The **Jasmine Tearooms**, in the main street, is a great place to go for tea or coffee and a delicious snack.

③ Continue downhill through open fields and three gates to reach **Coldharbour Farm**. Follow footpath signs left before the farmhouse then straight ahead on a grassy track, through a gate and downhill to reach the lane through another gate.

④ The EVW goes left here but we turn right up the lane to reach **Blight's Farm** (right). Turn left through a gate and up the track to **Surridge Farm**. Turn left through a big metal gate, then another at the

hilltop, continuing downhill through another gate onto a green lane (muddy in winter). There are views of **Morebath** ahead.

⑤ The lane joins a flinty track; turn left and over the dismantled railway towards **Ashtown Farm** then right down the drive under ancient lime trees. Turn right and follow the deep lane uphill past the **Old Vicarage** to the centre of Morebath.

⑥ Turn right down the B3190, taking care (there's no pavement). At **Bonny Cross** go right (signed '**Bampton**') to pass **Lodfin Cross** and the old station. When the road bends sharply right take the stony track straight ahead, slightly uphill.

⑦ At the hilltop a footpath sign leads right over a stile. Go down the field, over a stile then straight on, over a stile and through a gate at the top of the next field. Turn immediately left through another gate. Cross the field diagonally towards the left-hand gate at the top. Pass through the next two fields to a stile in the hedge at the top, then down a narrow fenced path towards **Bampton**. Cross over the next stile and field to gain the road over another stile.

⑧ Turn left, then cross over to take the old road into the town. Turn right and go straight ahead towards the church and your car.

> **WHAT TO LOOK FOR** ⓘ
> Beyond Point ⑦ of the walk you get your first sight of the Norman motte and bailey of **Bampton Castle** which was built on Saxon foundations in 1067. Traces of the original enclosure are still visible within the bailey, and Saxon strip system fields can still just be detected to the north east of the mound.

A Loop to the Exeter Inn

A relaxing stroll above the River Batherm to an old coaching hostelry.
See map and information panel for Walk 13

•DISTANCE•	8 miles (12.9km)
•MINIMUM TIME•	4hrs
•ASCENT / GRADIENT•	520ft (158m) ▲▲▲
•LEVEL OF DIFFICULTY•	🚶🚶 🚶🚶 🚶🚶

Walk 14 Directions (Walk 13 option)

If you feel like extending Walk 13 you can add on an easy loop to the 15th-century **Exeter Inn** to the south of **Bampton**.

Leave the main walk midway through Point ⑧ by passing the tourist information centre and turning left down **Silver Street**, then right, and immediately left into **Brook Street**. Ahead is the **Toll House** and old packhorse road (right). Follow the main A396 road, signposted 'ptinr**Tiverton**'. After 250yds (229m) take the first road left uphill to meet the edge of a wood.

A few steps later take the signposted footpath sharp left, then up the steps (right). Cross a stile into a field and turn left. Cross the fence in the next field and pass to the right of **Bowbierhill Farm**. Turn right after the next stile and, after a few steps, sharp left through a farm gate to reach a broad grassy track. Go through another farm gate (right) to climb steeply uphill to cross the stiles in the right-hand corner. Continue ahead, passing the remains of **Higher Bowbierhill** on the right. Go over the next stile and

right on the grassy track, with fine views over the Exe valley. Follow the track sloping downhill to join a sunken beech avenue.

At the T-junction in front of a house turn left onto a level, lawned area from which you enter an enclosed wooded footpath. This leads to the road; turn right (taking care) to reach the **Exeter Inn** after 1½ miles (2.4km). This is an excellent and welcoming real ale pub, popular with local country sportsmen, and serving a great range of food.

To return to **Bampton**, take the road opposite the pub and after a few paces take the second gate on the right. Cross the stile and go left around the field, leaving it over a stile by a gate. Turn right and the lane leads back to the car park.

WHILE YOU'RE THERE ℹ

Drive into Somerset to **Wimbleball Lake**, straight up the B3190 and over Haddon Hill beyond Morebath. Wimbleball – 374 acres (151ha) of water and 500 acres (202ha) of surrounding meadow and woodland – lies just inside the Exmoor National Park and there are plenty of recreational opportunities here: sailing and rowing clubs, a gift shop and café, a camping field and miles of waymarked trails, as well as a nature reserve.

Walk 15

The Historic Exeter to Topsham Canal

A stroll along the very first English canal to use locks – and a look at the old port of Topsham.

•DISTANCE•	4 miles (6.4km)
•MINIMUM TIME•	2hrs
•ASCENT / GRADIENT•	Negligible
•LEVEL OF DIFFICULTY•	
•PATHS•	Level tow paths
•LANDSCAPE•	River estuary; extensive mudflats at low tide
•SUGGESTED MAP•	aqua3 OS Explorer 110 Torquay & Dawlish
•START / FINISH•	Grid reference: SX 972844
•DOG FRIENDLINESS•	Watch out for wildlife – and mountain bikes
•PARKING•	By St Clement's Church, Powderham
•PUBLIC TOILETS•	Turf Hotel, Passage House Inn, by fire station in Topsham

Walk 15 Directions

This easy walk along the picturesque estuary of the River Exe has a huge amount to offer. You can visit medieval **Powderham Castle**, which is open to visitors from April to October (excluding Saturdays) and you can see the oldest ship canal in the country. There are usually boat trips to watch the rare avocets here in February – and a ferry ride takes you to the historic port of **Topsham**.

St Clement's Church, where you leave your car, is situated on the very edge of the **Powderham Estate**, the historic family home of the Earls of Devon. The original building dates back to the late 14th century when it was the home of Sir Philip Courtenay. Extensive damage caused during the Civil War was followed by a comprehensive programme of restoration in the 18th and 19th centuries.

The walk starts down the lane past the church towards the river. After a few paces turn left to join the **South West Way** (unmarked as such) which follows the **Exeter-to-Penzance railway** line here, running along the bank of the Exe estuary. Walk along the path to cross the railway. Turn left to walk upriver; there are superb views to (from left to right) Topsham, Exton, the Royal Marine Commandos Training Centre, Lympstone and Exmouth. Within 20 minutes you

WHILE YOU'RE THERE

If you feel like a change, it's quite possible to explore the Exe estuary and south Devon coastline without using your feet! **Stuart Line Cruises** operate from Exmouth, just south of Topsham, and run trips both upriver and along the coast towards Dawlish and Sidmouth. There's also a trip to Topsham, with a return journey to Exmouth by train, which runs along the very edge of the estuary with wonderful views across to Powderham Castle and Starcross village.

should reach the outlet of the **Exeter Ship Canal** at the **Turf Lock**, with the **Turf Hotel** beyond.

The original canal here – the first English lock canal – was begun in 1563, and ran from Exeter to Matford Brook. It was extended to Topsham in 1676, and then to the Turf, enabling trade vessels of over 300 tons to reach Exeter again (the estuary had silted up during the 14th century). In 1827 the Exeter to Topsham Canal was deepened and extended a further 2 miles (3.2km) to the Turf Lock, giving it a total length of 5¼ miles (8.4km). The building which now houses the Turf Hotel was probably built to accommodate visiting boat crews and their horses. The horses were used to pull the barges up the canal to Exeter.

The original lock gates can be seen beside the canal. Made of wood and weighing 15 tons, these were opened and closed by hand-operated winches, requiring enormous strength; they needed constant repair, and were replaced every 50 years. The gates currently in use are made of steel and are electronically operated.

Don't go over the lock gates here (unless you are in need of refreshment already!) but keep straight on up the canal. This stretch is beautiful, with bulrushes and waterlilies lining the banks, and is popular with canoeists. The only problem with the tow path here is that you are under constant threat from mountain bikers – but you can always catch the *White Heather*

WHERE TO EAT AND DRINK ⓘ

The Turf Hotel, in a fantastic position on a narrow point of land where the canal meets the River Exe, is a free house with excellent food – and no chips! Open from the start of April until early November, there are camping facilities here, making the most of its unique setting. The Passage House Inn by the ferry in Topsham specialises in seafood and welcomes families. It's a great place to sit outside and watch the goings on up and down the river.

---

launch for a change of scene (which operates daily from Exeter Quay to the Turf Hotel).

When you reach a small bridge over the canal, cross over to reach the **Topsham ferry slipway**. The ferry runs every day except Tuesday, April to September 11AM–5:30PM and at weekends and bank holidays October to March, but is always dependant on tide and weather. You can hail the ferryman if he's not already waiting for you. Catch the ferry over and have a drink at the **Passage House Inn** and, if you have time, take a look round **Topsham** itself. An important port since Roman times, it prospered greatly when shipping could no longer reach Exeter, and its eventful history has been based largely on shipbuilding and smuggling. Today life in Topsham is somewhat less dramatic. The estuary is used mainly by commercial and pleasure craft, and by thousands of birds who return each year to feed on the mudflats.

Finding your way back to your car from here should be fairly easy.

Walk 15

The Meandering Exe at Brampford Speke

Water-meadows, ox-bow lakes and herons – a post-Sunday-lunch amble along the riverbank of the Exe.

•DISTANCE•	3½ miles (5.7km)
•MINIMUM TIME•	1hr 30min
•ASCENT / GRADIENT•	Negligible
•LEVEL OF DIFFICULTY•	
•PATHS•	Grassy field paths, tracks and country lanes, 5 stiles
•LANDSCAPE•	Water-meadows and farmland
•SUGGESTED MAP•	aqua3 OS Explorer 114 Exeter & the Exe Valley
•START / FINISH•	Grid reference: SX 927986
•DOG FRIENDLINESS•	Livestock in some fields
•PARKING•	On laneside near St Peter's Church, Brampford Speke
•PUBLIC TOILETS•	None on route

BACKGROUND TO THE WALK

There is a secluded piece of Devonshire countryside lying just north of Exeter. Few would think of turning off the A377 Exeter to Crediton road to have a look around – but here is a beautiful area of undulating woods and farmland on the edge of the Exe Valley. Brampford Speke is just one of the pleasant cob and thatch villages that lies tucked away here, situated on a low cliff of red sandstone overhanging the River Exe as it meanders lazily through its flood plain. The Victorian writer George Gissing described the village:

> *'I have discovered a village called Brampford Speke on the Exe, which I seriously think is one of the most perfect I ever saw. One imagines that some lord of the manor must exert himself to keep it in a picturesque state.'*

That impression still holds true today – you almost feel as if the river is relieved to reach Brampford Speke and is taking a rest after a long journey from its source. This is high on Exmoor to the north, from where it tumbles down through deeply wooded combes, past the Norman castle at Tiverton, under the bridge at Bickleigh and onto the flood plain.

Ox-bow Lakes and Tucking Mills

As you stroll along the banks of the Exe you may notice a number of places where it appears that the river has changed – or is going to change – its course. This is a common flood plain feature. The erosive power of the water alters as the river swings through the level plain, and starts to cut deeply into the outer bends of its course. At the same time silt and alluvial debris carried in its waters are deposited on the inner bends where the current is less strong. As time goes on the process intensifies until eventually the river cuts across the bend and carves a new course, leaving behind a curved 'ox-bow' lake, separate from the river.

The fertile red soils of the Exe Valley, derived from Permian sandstones, provide good arable farmland and meadows, the best agricultural land in Devon. The area has been thickly populated and farmed for centuries. At Upton Pyne a group of Bronze Age burial barrows has been dated to around 2000 BC. It was recorded in the Domesday Book (1086) that of 99 mills in Devon, three-quarters were located in or east of the Exe Valley. This was an important cloth-making area in the 14th century, with a large number of fulling ('tucking') mills (where woven cloth was flattened to improve its appearance). A tax return of 1332 recorded that 38 'tuckers' were sufficiently well off to pay tax, and that a large percentage came from this area.

Walk 16 Directions

① Follow the **Exe Valley Way** (EVW) footpath signs through the churchyard round to the left of the church. Leave via a metal gate, and follow the narrow path on through a kissing gate. The path brings you out onto a lane at a wooden kissing gate under a lychgate.

② Turn right and follow the footpath signs downhill to cross the **River Exe** over a large wooden bridge. Turn left across the meadow, following the footpath signs. Note the old station and stationmaster's house (now private) on the right. Ignore the footpath signpost pointing right and go through a gateway in the hedge, keeping close to the river (on your left).

Walk 16

③ Follow the river as it loops around the flood plain. Cross the old railway line via two kissing gates. On the left you can see the old railway bridge piers in the river.

④ Immediately through the second gate drop down left to the river and continue straight on. Cross a stile, then a double stile; then a second double stile with a plank bridge.

WHAT TO LOOK FOR

You're quite likely to get a sight of a **grey heron** during this walk. This large, but graceful, long-legged wader is unmistakable, but always exciting to see, whether waiting patiently for prey – which it swallows whole – near shallow water, or flying off with its neck drawn back and legs trailing. The heron can stand or perch without moving for long periods of time, and can grow to as much as 36in (91cm) tall.

⑤ After a mile (1.6km) the path veers right away from the river and down a green lane to a kissing gate. Turn immediately left along another green lane. At the next footpath post go right, then straight on (ignoring EVW signs left) along a green lane. The hedges disappear and the lane crosses arable farmland, ending at a road on the edge of **Rewe**.

⑥ Turn right along the lane towards **Stoke Canon** to pass the old cross at **Burrow Farm**. Carry straight on to pass **Oakhay Barton**. Note the Stoke Canon level crossing on the Exeter–Tiverton line ahead.

⑦ Just before the level crossing follow the footpath sign right through a kissing gate and along a fenced path. Pass through another kissing gate and metal gate to join a dismantled railway line.

WHERE TO EAT AND DRINK

The **Agricultural Inn** (free house) in the centre of Brampford Speke welcomes families, serves very good food and has an attractive outdoor seating area. It is also the meeting point for Aerosaurus and Exeter Balloons, who muster here to decide on the best place to fly, depending on the weather conditions at the time.

Pass through another kissing gate and straight on. The **River Exe** loops in on the left and **Brampford Speke church** is seen ahead above the river – it's a beautifully serene spot. A kissing gate leads over a small bridge and into a copse. Another kissing gate leads back into the meadows (marshy in winter, but there is a small wooden footbridge, right, for use at such times) and to the footbridge over the Exe.

⑧ Once you're over the bridge, retrace your steps up the path, turning left at the lychgate and then back through the churchyard to your car.

WHILE YOU'RE THERE

Have a day out in historic **Exeter**, 3 miles (4.8km) south of Brampford Speke. Although heavily damaged by bombing in May 1942, the city has much to recommend it. Situated at the lowest crossing point of the River Exe, the Romans established a settlement here – Isca – around AD 50, and traces of the original Roman walls (c AD 200) can be seen today. The Norman period is represented by Rougemont Castle (1068), and the superb cathedral and close (1114–33), with its intricately carved West Front and unique ribbed, vaulted ceiling above the nave. From the 10th to 18th centuries Exeter was a port of some significance, and the recently restored quay and associated wharves and warehouses provide an attractive setting for cafés and craft shops.

A Dartmoor Outlier Above the Teign Valley

Daffodils at Steps Bridge – a climb up Heltor Rock en route for Bridford – and a very special church.

•DISTANCE•	5 miles (8km)
•MINIMUM TIME•	2hrs 45min
•ASCENT / GRADIENT•	393ft (120m) ▲▲▲
•LEVEL OF DIFFICULTY•	🚶🚶 🚶🚶 🚶
•PATHS•	Woodland paths, open fields and country lanes, 7 stiles
•LANDSCAPE•	Steeply wooded valleys and undulating farmland
•SUGGESTED MAP•	aqua3 OS Explorer 110 Torquay & Dawlish
•START / FINISH•	Grid reference: SX 804883
•DOG FRIENDLINESS•	Keep under control in the woods, livestock in some fields
•PARKING•	Free car park (and tourist information) at Steps Bridge
•PUBLIC TOILETS•	At car park, Bridford Inn and Steps Bridge café

BACKGROUND TO THE WALK

In early springtime many people travel out to Steps Bridge (built in 1816) to stroll along the River Teign, enjoying the sight of thousands of tiny wild daffodils crowding the riverbanks. But there's a better way to explore this valley, which includes a close look at an example of that most characteristic Dartmoor feature, a tor, and a pint at one of the Teign Valley's best pubs as an added bonus!

The Teign Valley Woodlands

Much of the ancient semi-natural woodland and valley meadows around Steps Bridge is a Site of Special Scientific Interest (SSSI), and many acres are owned by the National Trust. Dunsford Wood (on the opposite bank of the Teign from the car park) is managed as a nature reserve by the Devon Wildlife Trust. These woodlands are glorious all year round: there are snowdrops in February, daffodils in early spring, wood anemones and ramsoms; then foxgloves, woodrush and cow-wheat in summer. Look out for the nest of the wood ant by the side of the path, which can be as much as a metre high. If you place your cheek or hand near to a nest you'll get a shock – the ants squirt formic acid from their abdomens in a defensive move, and it stings!

On the Edge of Dartmoor

Blackingstone Rock is another outlying tor, 1 mile (1.6km) south west of Heltor Rock. Turn right rather than left at Point ④ and you will soon be aware of its huge, granite mass rising above the lane on the left. You can get to the top by climbing up an almost vertical flight of steps which were added in the 19th century for that purpose. The views of the surrounding countryside are worth the effort.

While you're in Bridford, part way round the walk, it's well worthwhile going inside the church. The original chapel on this site was dedicated by Bishop Bronescombe in 1259, to the murdered Archibishop Thomas à Becket, who died at Canterbury Cathedral in 1170.

This was still a common practice in many West Country churches during the century following his death. The present building dates from the 15th century, and its most famous feature is the superb eight-bay rood screen, thought to date from 1508. The faces of the richly carved and coloured figures were mutilated by Puritan soldiers during the Civil War, but what survives is still impressive. The doors are also unusual in that they are made in one piece rather than being divided in the middle. These details are often overlooked by the Steps Bridge hordes.

Walk 17 Directions

① Cross the road, following the signs to the **youth hostel**. Turn right up the concrete track, then left. When you reach the **youth hostel** turn right again, this time following signs for **Heltor Farm**. The steep path leads uphill through delightful oak, then beech woodland. At a T-junction of paths turn left and up over some wooden steps by the gate into a field.

② Follow wooden footpath posts straight up the field. Go through the metal gate, then between granite gateposts; look right to see **Heltor Rock**. Pass signs for **Lower Heltor Farm** at a metal gate onto a green lane; turn left.

Walk 17

③ Follow the footpath signs left then right round the farmhouse to meet a track. Turn left up the farm drive, which becomes a tarmac lane.

④ At the top of the lane turn left (signs for **Bridford**). After 200yds (183m) turn left over a stile up the narrow fenced permissive path to **Heltor**, from where you can enjoy an amazing panorama. Retrace your steps to the road and turn left.

⑤ The lane eventually bends left, then right, to reach the edge of **Bridford**. Turn right down a small steep lane signed 'Parish Hall & Church'. Follow the path round the churchyard, down steps and right to find the **Bridford Inn**.

⑥ Turn left from the pub and follow the lane through the centre of the village. Take the third lane (**Neadon Lane**) on the right, by a telephone box. Just past where a bridleway joins (from the left) the lane dips to the right, downhill; take the left fork ahead to pass **Westbirch Farm** on the right. Turn left at the track to **Birch Down Farm**. Continue over two stiles by the barn and across the field, keeping the wire fence to your right. Go over the stile and up the right-hand edge of the next field to a stile in the top corner. Then cross over a tumbledown granite wall and carry straight on through an area of gorse bushes, heading towards a footpath signpost. Cross a stile by some beech trees.

⑦ Continue along the top of the field, through two metal gates and down a green lane to reach **Lower Lowton Farm**. Turn right to a footpath signpost, and follow the bridleway right (signed 'Woodlands'). Keep to the bridleway past a new looking barn on the left, then turn right through a wooden gate and downhill on a narrow green lane. Cross a track between the fields via two gates, then through a small wooden gate. Continue down the deeply banked green lane until you reach a surfaced lane.

⑧ Turn left through the middle gate, signed 'Byway to Steps Bridge'. At the edge of **Bridford Wood** (by the National Trust sign) turn right following the footpath signposts. The path is fairly narrow and quite steep. Go left, then right, to cross a sandy track, keeping downhill. The path then runs to the left, now high above the river to **Steps Bridge** where it meets the road opposite the café. Turn left here to return to your car.

Around Lustleigh Cleave

A hard – yet rewarding – exploration of the wooded Bovey Valley.

•DISTANCE•	5 miles (8km)
•MINIMUM TIME•	3hrs
•ASCENT / GRADIENT•	754ft (230m) ▲▲▲
•LEVEL OF DIFFICULTY•	👫 👫 👫
•PATHS•	Steep rocky ascents/descents, rough paths and woodland
•LANDSCAPE•	Deeply wooded river valley and open moorland
•SUGGESTED MAP•	aqua3 OS Outdoor Leisure 28 Dartmoor
•START / FINISH•	Grid reference: SX 774815
•DOG FRIENDLINESS•	Dogs can run free but take care with livestock
•PARKING•	By side of lane at Hammerslake
•PUBLIC TOILETS•	Kes Tor Inn at Water

BACKGROUND TO THE WALK

Lustleigh is one of those perfect Devon villages that everyone just has to see. The rose-covered cottages and pub cluster tightly around the green and 13th-century Church of St John the Baptist. The quintessentially English cricket field, rushing streams and boulder-strewn hillslopes, all nestling together in a deep wooded valley beneath the eastern fringe of Dartmoor, make this a real magnet. But Lustleigh has a problem (or perhaps an advantage?) – there is no car park, meaning that many people weave their way through the cars parked around the church and drive off again in frustration. But there is another way of getting a feel for the real Lustleigh: drive on through the village, park, and walk back in.

On a Clear Day…
From the ridge approaching Hunter's Tor (after Point ②) you get a superb 360-degree view. To the south you can see the coast at Teignmouth. Following around clockwise you can pick out the familiar outline of Haytor, then Hound Tor (resembling a pack of hounds frozen in flight), Hayne Down and Bowerman's Nose, Manaton church and rocks, Easdon Tor, North Bovey, the Manor House Hotel, then Moretonhampstead with Mardon Down behind. Continuing round there is the stark outline of Blackingstone Rock then, far beyond on the Haldon Hills, the white tower of Haldon Belvedere, a folly erected in 1770 by Sir Robert Palk in memory of Major General Stringer Lawrence, the 'father of the Indian army'.

Lustleigh still holds a traditional May Day ceremony, which takes place on the first Saturday in May. The festival had died out, but was revived in the early years of the 20th century by Cecil Torr who, while living at Wreyland, wrote his famous three-volume work *Small Talk at Wreyland*, a charming record of rural life. The crowning ceremony at that time took place at Long Tor on the outskirts of the village. The May Queen, dressed in white and garlanded with spring flowers (and elected from the local children – candidates must have danced around the maypole on at least five previous occasions) leads a procession around the village beneath a canopy of flowers which is held aloft by other Lustleigh children. She is then crowned on the May Day rock in the Town Orchard. A new granite throne was set in place on the rock to celebrate the Millennium, and the names of recent May Queens are carved below.

½ Mile
1 km

④
PECK FARM
HUNTER'S TOR
FOXWORTHY BRIDGE ⑤
FOXWORTHY
③ IRON AGE FORT
▲326
Raven's Tor
HORSHAM
NATURE RESERVE
⑥ HORSHAM STEPS
KES TOR INN
WC
LETCHOLE PLANTATION
▲215
R Bovey
⑧ WATER
⑦
LUSTLEIGH CLEAVE
CLAM BRIDGE
② HAMMERSLAKE
Woodash
Sharpitor
262▲
P
GROVE ①
Earthwork
Hut Circles
LOGANSTONES
Houndtor Wood
WAYE FARM
PETHYBRIDGE
Ⓐ
WOODLAND TRUST LAND
Lustleigh
Trendlebere Down
HISLEY BRIDGE
HISLEY
Gradner Rocks
Ⓑ
Ⓒ
WREYLAND
WREYLAND MANOR
WRAY BROOK
BOVEY VALLEY WOODLANDS
DISMANTLED RAILWAY

Walk 18 Directions

① With **Lustleigh** village behind you, walk straight ahead from your car and turn left up a narrow rocky path between the houses '**Loganstones**' and '**Grove**', following bridleway signs '**Cleave for Water**'. At the gate go straight ahead signed '**Hunter's Tor**' and climb steeply up to the top, where there are wide views over the moor.

② Turn right through oak woodland; the vegetation clears, and you follow the path straight on over the highest part of the ridge (1,063ft/324m) and across the remains of the Iron Age fort to reach **Hunter's Tor**.

③ Pass through the gate right of the tor and follow the signed path right to meet another signed path left. Follow the track downhill through one gate, then immediately right through another and downhill towards **Peck Farm**. Go through the gate and straight on down the concrete drive.

④ Shortly after turn left through a gate signed to '**Foxworthy Bridge**' and continue along a wooded track. Pass through two gates to reach the beautiful thatched hamlet at **Foxworthy**; turn right.

⑤ Almost immediately go left, signed '**Horsham**'. Follow the track into mixed woodland through a gate. After 5 minutes or so follow signs right for '**Horsham for Manaton & Water**', to reach the **River Bovey**. Follow the riverbank left for a few paces to the crossing (on boulders) at **Horsham Steps**. **Note:** If you are concerned about crossing the river at Horsham Steps,

don't turn left for 'Horsham' at Point ⑤, go right down the drive, which crosses the river. Take the first footpath left and follow the river until you rejoin the main route at Point ⑥.

⑥ Cross over, taking care, to enter a nature reserve. Follow the path steeply uphill through woodland and over a stile. Keep left at two junctions then pass through a gate by two pretty cottages (note the tree-branch porch) following signs for '**Water**' through **Letchhole Plantation**.

⑦ At the crossroads of tracks turn right ('**Manaton direct**') to meet the lane by cottages at **Water**. Take the second lane right to the **Kes Tor Inn**.

⑧ Retrace your steps to the crossroads. Go straight on downhill to a split in the track. Keep left through a gate and continue down the steep, stony path (signed '**Clam Bridge for Lustleigh Cleave**'). Cross the river on the split-log bridge and proceed steeply uphill to the signpost left '**Lustleigh via Hammerslake**'. Go left and left again at the next signpost (very steep). Pass a large granite boulder and follow the signs for **Hammerslake**. At the gate turn right down the rocky path back to the lane at the start.

WHERE TO EAT AND DRINK ⓘ
The **Kes Tor Inn** at Water has a range of bar snacks. On summer afternoons cream teas are often served at **Manaton village hall**, near the church. The thatched 15th-century **Cleave Inn** at Lustleigh has a delightful garden and serves excellent food. The **Primrose Cottage Tearooms** provide the perfect setting for a Devon cream tea.

A Look at Lustleigh Village

A less taxing way through Lustleigh Cleave – and a return through Wreyland.
See map and information panel for Walk 18

Walk 19

•DISTANCE•	4 miles (6.4km)
•MINIMUM TIME•	2hrs
•ASCENT / GRADIENT•	460ft (140m) ▲▲▲
•LEVEL OF DIFFICULTY•	👫 👫 👫

Walk 19 Directions
(Walk 18 option)

If you'd prefer a slightly easier alternative to Walk 18, and want to see the village itself, this will suit you better, but it's still quite tough.

Walk back along the lane towards **Lustleigh**. Pass **Waye Farm**, and shortly after turn right up a stony track signed '**Lustleigh Cleave**', Point Ⓐ. Pass through **Heaven's Gate** and proceed downhill into the valley. Turn left into Woodland Trust land. Follow grassy paths to a track at the bottom of the hill.

Turn left through conifers, past the ivy-covered ruins of **Boveycombe Farm**, to reach a fork. Go right towards the old packhorse bridge at **Hisley**, Point Ⓑ. Don't cross over; turn left and follow the river over a stile into the **Bovey Valley Woodlands**. Cross a second stile along the riverbank, pass through a gate and across the field to join a lane at a metal gate.

Turn left uphill and take the first lane right. Soon take the footpath signed '**Wreyland**' right, Point Ⓒ. Follow the path to cross the bridge over **Wray Brook**. Go left (note the old railway viaduct on the left) and follow the signs along the field edge then through a gate into **Wreyland**.

Turn left to pass **Wreyland Manor** (dating from the 1360s, but altered in 1680) and cricket pitch and enter **Lustleigh** by the green, the oldest part, with its stone cross erected in memory of Henry Tudor, rector 1888-1904. Turn left at the church and go straight ahead between the dairy and post office into the **Town Orchard**. Carry on past the May Day rock to the end of the orchard and cross the leat on a wooden bridge. Go through the gate and, at the next junction of paths, drop down right to see the magical granite 'footbridge'.

Retrace your steps to the junction and go straight over to join the lane. Turn left, then first right to zig-zag very steeply up a lane to **Pethybridge**, between two thatched cottages. Turn left, then right at the top. Walk past **Waye Farm** and return to your car.

WHILE YOU'RE THERE ⓘ

Becka Falls are just south of Manaton on the Bovey Tracey road. This natural waterfall, where the Becka Brook tumbles more than 80ft (24m) over a succession of huge granite boulders, is at its most impressive after heavy rainfall.

Walk 20

The Rocky Teign Gorge to Fingle Bridge

Follow the Teign through the Castle Drogo estate – known as the 'youngest' castle in the country.

•DISTANCE•	4 miles (6.4km)
•MINIMUM TIME•	2hrs
•ASCENT / GRADIENT•	Negligible ▲▲▲
•LEVEL OF DIFFICULTY•	👫 👫 👫
•PATHS•	Riverside paths and tracks, one steep stony section, 2 stiles
•LANDSCAPE•	Deeply wooded river gorge and meadows
•SUGGESTED MAP•	aqua3 OS Outdoor Leisure 28 Dartmoor
•START / FINISH•	Grid reference: SX 713894
•DOG FRIENDLINESS•	Dogs should be kept under control in woodlands
•PARKING•	Over Dogmarsh Bridge on A382 (beyond Mill End Hotel)
•PUBLIC TOILETS•	At Anglers Rest

Walk 20 Directions

Castle Drogo, built in local granite between 1910 and 1930, occupies a spectacular position high above the Teign Gorge near Drewsteignton in north east Dartmoor. Given to the National Trust by the Drewe family in 1974, it was designed by Sir Edwin Lutyens and has the honour of being the 'youngest' castle in the country. Self-made millionaire Julius Drewe established his family seat here because of a romantic notion that his ancestors had connections with the village, but he did not live to see his dream fully completed. In 2000 the Trust introduced a scheme locally to create innovative outdoor sculptures based on Lutyens' design for a gateway – Julius Drewe had lost heart in the idea after his eldest son Adrian died in World War I.

This walk takes you through the edge of the Drogo estate along the

sparkling upper River Teign and, apart from one rocky section (avoidable so long as the river is low), is fairly easy.

Walk back towards the bridge, then left through the kissing gate, following the footpath sign 'Two Moors Way' to enter the **Castle Drogo Estate**. Walk along the placid river through broad meadows, and through two kissing gates. **Castle Drogo** can be seen above left, and the steep-sided **Teign Gorge** ahead.

WHAT TO LOOK FOR ⓘ

Look up above Fingle Bridge and you will see the precipitously steep slopes leading up to the site of **Prestonbury Castle** Iron Age hillfort, facing its counterpart **Cranbrook Castle** on the other side of the valley These two impressive sites, built by Celtic peoples to guard the Teign Gorge, provide evidence of relatively sophisticated habitation in the area as long ago as 750 BC – over 2,000 years before Julius Drewe's dream came to fruition.

Walk 20

Go over a stile and small footbridge into oak woodland. Follow the **Fisherman's Path** signs straight on along the left bank. An iron bridge over the river right marks the return route. The **Two Moors Way** goes left here. Walk straight on past a broad pool and weir, part of the castle's hydro-electric scheme.

The narrow, mossy path, at times rocky, proceeds along the gorge. It's incredibly pretty at all times of year, and particularly glorious in autumn. The path undulates gently. Down in the river there are rocky islands, fast-flowing, tumbling sections, and deep clear pools where the river takes on a lazy feel – and lots of good places for picnics and toe-dipping, or where you can sit and contemplate the scene. Soon the old pumping station comes into view on

the opposite bank. A little later the path splits. If the water is low go straight ahead over a rocky section that floods easily in winter. If that is impassable, or if you feel like gaining a little height, climb the big, steep stone steps left to pass up and over a rocky outcrop.

A small flight of wooden steps leads you up to the preferred path, so avoiding riverbank erosion. Pass through a small hunting gate to gain a weir, with benches – a great place to picnic. Just beyond that the valley widens to form a broad grassy area opposite. Ahead you can see the steep slopes of **Prestonbury Castle** Iron Age hillfort above Fingle Bridge. It looks across the gorge to its twin, **Cranbrook Castle**, on the hilltop opposite.

Fingle Bridge and the **Anglers Rest** are reached after 2 miles (3.2km). Cross the old packhorse bridge and turn right (signs to **Hannicombe Wood**) to return on the track which runs parallel to the river. This is fairly level and passes through mixed deciduous then coniferous woodland; very soon you're on your own again.

When a small path leads right from the track take a moment to go and have a look at the pumping station and leat leading from the weir below the castle. Rejoin the main track, pass through a five-bar gate and walk past a superb 8ft (2.5m) granite wall, then right over stone steps to pass down and over the iron bridge to the other bank, to rejoin the route out. Turn left, over the stile into the meadows, and back to your car.

The Dartmoor National Park Authority at Bovey Tracey

The River Bovey woodlands and the old Newton Abbot-to-Moretonhampstead railway line.

•DISTANCE•	3 miles (4.8km)
•MINIMUM TIME•	1hr 30min
•ASCENT / GRADIENT•	196ft (60m) ▲▲ ▲ ▲
•LEVEL OF DIFFICULTY•	🚶🚶 🚶🚶 🚶🚶
•PATHS•	Woodland and field paths, 4 stiles
•LANDSCAPE•	Wooded river valley and parkland
•SUGGESTED MAP•	aqua3 OS Explorer 110 Torquay & Dawlish
•START / FINISH•	Grid reference: SX 814782
•DOG FRIENDLINESS•	Dogs should be kept under control at all times
•PARKING•	Car park on the B3344 at lower end of Fore Street, Bovey Tracey, with tourist information office
•PUBLIC TOILETS•	At car park

BACKGROUND TO THE WALK

The road signs as you approach Bovey Tracey proudly proclaim the town as being the 'Gateway to the Moor', and although this may be debatable (the town is 3 miles/4.8km from the open moor, and gives no impression of Dartmoor proper) it is certainly true that the character of the landscape changes markedly as you leave the town. To the west the road climbs steadily up towards the tourist honeypot of Hay Tor, and the northern route travels past picturesque Lustleigh through the wooded Wray valley to reach Moretonhampstead and the open moorland beyond. The town's other claim to fame is that it is home to the headquarters of the Dartmoor National Park Authority, based at Parke, a splendid house set in spacious parkland just to the west of the town. The River Bovey runs through the National Trust's Parke Estate, and the area provides an excellent range of walking opportunities.

Rails to Trails

The 12-mile (19.3km) Newton Abbot-to-Moretonhampstead railway line was opened in 1866, and finally closed for passenger traffic in 1959. A group of enthusiasts tried to keep it open as a preserved steam line, but were unsuccessful. Attempts are being made at the time of writing to open the line as a walking and cycling route. It was closed for goods traffic to Moretonhampstead in 1964, and to Bovey Tracey in 1970. The line is still laid as track as far as Heathfield, 2 miles (3.2km) south of Bovey Tracey, and is opened to the public on special occasions.

Parke Estate

The building housing the National Park's offices at Parke was built around 1826 on the site of a derelict Tudor house, and left to the National Trust by Major Hole in 1974. In 1999 the eleven National Parks of England and Wales celebrated the 50th anniversary of the legislation that established them. The Dartmoor National Park, covering 368 sq miles (953 sq km), was number four (in October 1951), following the Peak District, the Lake District and Snowdonia. Walkers should appreciate the purposes behind the National Parks movement – 'the conservation of the natural beauty, wildlife and cultural heritage of the area, and the promotion of the understanding and enjoyment of its special qualities by the public'. The office at Parke is open for enquiries during normal office hours and is a useful port of call before planning any walks on Dartmoor.

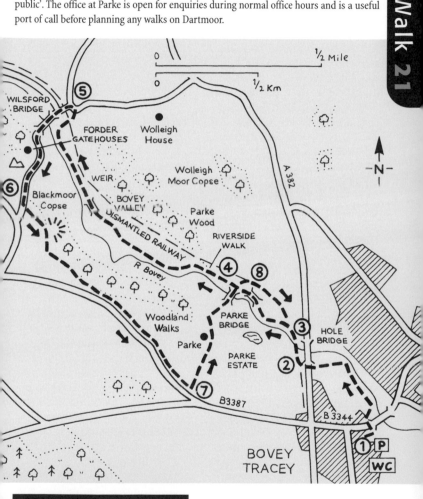

Walk 21 Directions

① Cross the road and turn right, following the signs for 'Town centre shops'. Just before you come to the the bridge turn left along a concrete walkway into **Mill Marsh Park**, past the children's playground and through the arboretum. This level footpath leads past the sports field

to meet the busy A382 at **Hole Bridge** via a kissing gate. Cross the road carefully.

② Go through the kissing gate and turn right to enter the **National Trust's Parke Estate** on the trackbed of the, now dismantled, Newton Abbot-to-Moretonhampstead railway line. Follow the path over the **Bovey**.

③ Turn immediately left down wooden steps and over a stile to follow the river (left). Cross a stile at the end of the field and carry on through a wooded strip, down wooden steps and over a footbridge and stile into the next field.

④ Signs here point left for **Parke** and right for '**Railway Walk**' but you should go straight on following the '**Riverside Walk**' through the field into woodland, then on a raised wooden walkway to the river. The path winds on, then runs along between woods with fields on the right, then over a footbridge to meet the river at a weir. Follow the bank, ignoring a broad track right. Two kissing gates lead out of National Trust land and past a footbridge on the left. A few paces later the footpath turns right to cross the railway track. Turn left and straight on to a lane via a kissing gate.

⑤ Turn left (signed '**Manaton**') and pass between the old railway bridge piers. Walk across **Wilsford Bridge**, ignoring signs to **Lustleigh** right. Continue up the lane past **Forder gatehouses**, then steeply uphill until the lane bends sharp right.

⑥ Turn left over a stile to re-enter the **Parke Estate**. The wooded path is narrow, with views left over the Bovey Valley. Go through a beech

---

WHILE YOU'RE THERE ⓘ

Visit the **Devon Guild of Craftsmen**, which can be found just by the bridge over the Bovey by the car park. Open every day (except winter bank holidays) from 10AM–5:30PM, this is a wonderful place to go and browse for presents in the craft shop, where you can see a huge range of items produced by local craftspeople. There is also a gallery upstairs, where the Guild puts on special themed exhibitions.

---

wood and kissing gate to enter a large field. Keep to the right edge, dropping gradually downhill, to leave via a kissing gate and down a narrow wooded path parallel to the road.

⑦ The path ends at a kissing gate; turn sharp left to walk across the parkland and the drive to Parke car park. Walk downhill to cross the lower drive, then left to walk below the house, ending at a five-bar gate. Turn right ('**Riverside Walk**') to cross the river at **Parke Bridge**, then straight on to join the old railway track.

⑧ Turn right and follow the track until it crosses the **Bovey**, to meet the A382. Cross the road to enter **Mill Marsh Park** and retrace your steps to your car.

WHERE TO EAT AND DRINK ⓘ

The **Old Thatched Inn** can be found on the left as you leave the car park. This 17th-century coaching inn is a free house and has accommodation. The **Devon Guild of Craftsmen** has a café offering all kinds of delicious food and drink, and an attractive courtyard seating area. There are also several cafés and pubs in Bovey Tracey itself.

WHAT TO LOOK FOR ⓘ

Look out for the charismatic **dipper** as you stroll along the riverbank. This usually solitary little bird can often be seen bobbing about the rocks in the river. It has a white throat and breast and chestnut underparts, and a characteristic peculiar to the species – it can walk and swim underwater in fast-flowing streams, searching for food. The force of the water on its slanted back as it walks along the streambed, with its head down, holds it on the bottom.

The Vision That is Dartington

A gentle walk around the Dartington Hall Estate, with a pretty pub loop along the steam railway.

•DISTANCE•	5 miles (8km)
•MINIMUM TIME•	2hrs 30min
•ASCENT / GRADIENT•	164ft (50m) ▲ ▲ ▲
•LEVEL OF DIFFICULTY•	👫 👫 👫
•PATHS•	Fields, woodland tracks and country lanes, 4 stiles
•LANDSCAPE•	River meadows, parkland and mixed woodland
•SUGGESTED MAP•	aqua3 OS Explorer 110 Torquay & Dawlish
•START / FINISH•	Grid reference: SX 799628
•DOG FRIENDLINESS•	Possibility of livestock in some fields; dogs (except guide dogs) not allowed within Dartington Hall grounds
•PARKING•	Opposite entrance to Dartington Hall
•PUBLIC TOILETS•	Outside entrance to Dartington Hall and Staverton village

BACKGROUND TO THE WALK

You could be forgiven for thinking that Dartington is really nothing more than what you see as you cross the roundabout on the A382 leading south from the A38 to Totnes – just somewhere you pass en route to the South Hams. But there's so much more to Dartington than that, and the story behind 'the vision' of Leonard and Dorothy Elmhirst, who bought the estate in 1925, is a fascinating one. This walk circles the estate and you should allow time at the end to visit its central buildings.

The Most Spectacular Medieval Mansion

Dartington Hall was described by Nikolaus Pevsner in his classic book on the buildings of Devon as 'the most spectacular medieval mansion' in Devon. The great hall and main courtyard were built for John Holland, Duke of Exeter, at the end of the 14th century, and although all the buildings have since been carefully restored, to walk through the gateway into the courtyard today, with the superb Great Hall with its hammerbeam roof opposite, is to step back in time. Arthur Champernowne came to own the manor in 1554, and made various alterations, and the estate stayed in the hands of the Champernowne family until 1925. Further restoration work was carried out in Georgian times, but by the time the Elmhirsts came on the scene the Hall was derelict. Modern visitors are welcome to explore the Great Hall, courtyard and gardens, providing they are not in use, in return for a moderate contribution per person.

St Mary's Church can be found on the northern edge of the estate just off the Totnes road. You'll pass the site of the original estate church just to the north of the Hall. It was demolished in 1873, leaving only the tower, which can be seen today. The new church, which is wonderfully light and spacious, was built in 1880, following the exact dimensions of the original building, and re-using various items from it, such as the south porch with its lovely star vault, the chancel screen, font, pulpit and roof. A tablet in the outer east wall records the rebuilding and subsequent consecration of the church by Frederick, Bishop of Exeter. The Dartington Hall Trust, a registered charity, was set up in 1935, and evolved from the vision of Leonard Elmhirst and his American wife Dorothy Whitney Straight, who bought the derelict hall and 1,000 acres (405ha) of the estate and set about making their dream reality. He was interested in farming and forestry, and in increasing employment opportunities in rural areas. She believed passionately in the arts as a way of promoting personal and social improvement. Their joint aim was to provide a foundation where both dreams could be realised simultaneously, and Dartington Hall today, home to Dartington College of Arts and a whole range of other educational facilities, provides the perfect setting.

Walk 22 Directions

① From the car park turn left downhill. Follow the pavement until you reach the **River Dart**.

② Turn left over a stile (no footpath sign) and follow the river

northwards. This part of the walk is likely to be very muddy after rainfall. The Dart here is broad, tree-lined and slow-moving. Pass over a stile, through a strip of woodland and over another stile into the next meadow. At the end of that pass over a stile onto a short wooded track.

Walk 22

WHILE YOU'RE THERE
Spend some time at the **Cider Press Centre**. This is a wonderful place to browse and shop. There's farm food, a stationery and bookshop, woodturning, great refreshments, a cookshop, Dartington pottery shop, toy shop and plant centre. It's the perfect place for present shopping all year round. Open seven days a week, and parking is free.

③ Walk along the river edge of the next field (with **Park Copse** to your left). At the end of that field cross a stile into **Staverton Ford Plantation**. Where the track veers sharply left go through the gate in the wall ahead, then right to follow a narrow, wooded path back towards the river. Keep on this path as it runs parallel with the **Dart**, becoming a broad woodland track through **North Wood**. When you see buildings through the trees on the right, leave the track and walk downhill to a metal gate and a lane.

④ Turn right to cross **Staverton Bridge**. At the level crossing turn right to pass through **Staverton Station** yard into a park-like area between the railway and river. Follow the path across the single-track railway and walk on to meet a lane by **Sweet William Cottage**.

⑤ Turn right and follow the lane to its end. Go straight ahead on a small gritty path to pass the **Church of St Paul de Leon**, who was a

9th-century travelling preacher. Turn left at the lane to pass the public toilets, and left at the junction to the **Sea Trout Inn**. After your break retrace your steps to the metal gate past **Staverton Bridge**.

⑥ Turn immediately right to rejoin the track. Follow this until it runs downhill and bends left. Walk towards the gate on the right, then turn left on the narrow concrete path. The houses of **Huxham's Cross** can be seen right. Keep on the concrete path, which leaves the woodland to run between wire fences to meet a concrete drive at the **Dartington Crafts Education Centre**. Follow the drive to meet the road.

⑦ Turn left to pass **Old Parsonage Farm**. Keep on the road back to **Dartington Hall**, passing the gardens and ruins of the original church (right), until you see the car park on the left.

WHAT TO LOOK FOR
You can't fail to notice the steam trains running along the opposite side of the river. This is the **South Devon Railway**, which runs from Buckfastleigh to Totnes. Staverton Station has featured in many television programmes and films, such as *The Railway Children*. The station at Buckfastleigh has old locomotives and rolling stock on display, a museum and café, riverside walks and a picnic area. Nearby is **Buckfast Butterflies and Otter Sanctuary**.

WHERE TO EAT AND DRINK
The thatched and beamed **Cott Inn** (established in 1320) is signposted from the roundabout in Dartington village and has a pretty garden, accommodation and good food. There are two excellent eateries at Dartington Cider Press Centre – **Cranks** vegetarian restaurant, and **Muffins**, which provides light lunches in the open air. Within the grounds of Dartington Hall there is the **White Hart** restaurant and bar, where you can enjoy a drink in atmospheric surroundings. The 15th-century **Sea Trout Inn** at Staverton has very good food, and was known as the Church House until 30 years ago, when it was renamed by the landlord in celebration of a successful fishing trip on the Dart.

Walk 23

3,500 Years on Dartmoor

From Bronze Age Grimspound to the Golden Dagger tin mine.

•DISTANCE•	6 miles (9.7km)
•MINIMUM TIME•	3hrs 15min
•ASCENT / GRADIENT•	656ft (200m) ▲▲ ▲▲ ▲
•LEVEL OF DIFFICULTY•	🚶 🚶 🚶
•PATHS•	Heathery tracks and grassy paths, 3 stiles
•LANDSCAPE•	Open moorland; sweeping valleys and ridges
•SUGGESTED MAP•	aqua3 OS Outdoor Leisure 28 Dartmoor
•START / FINISH•	Grid reference: SX 682819
•DOG FRIENDLINESS•	Watch out for livestock
•PARKING•	Small unmarked quarry on left of B3212
•PUBLIC TOILETS•	Warren House Inn, none on route

BACKGROUND TO THE WALK

The area around Vitifer and Birch Tor, near where you park, is a Site of Special Scientific Interest (SSSI), being one of the most spectacular areas of mature heather on Dartmoor, and rich in archaeological remains. Vitifer and Birch Tor mines, with Golden Dagger, were the only three large mines still producing tin in the 1820s, and by the mid-19th century Vitifer was employing over 100 men. It closed in 1870 due to falling demand for tin, but reopened in 1900 until 1914. A quantity of iron was also produced from the mines here.

Tin Mining on the Moor

Bennett's Cross is a slanting stone cross marking the line of the ancient track across the moor, followed today by the route of the B3212, which was constructed towards the end of the 18th century. The cross also marks the boundary between the mines at Vitifer and Headland Warren, and between the parishes of Chagford and North Bovey. It may have been named after a 16th-century tin miner.

The valley between Soussons Down and Challacombe Down has been the scene of industrial activity for over 800 years, although the name 'Golden Dagger' wasn't recorded until the 1850s. Medieval tinners extracted ore from the stream beds but later workers carried out open-cast mining, creating the deep gullies that are so obvious today. The whole area is cut and grooved under its covering of purple heather. Tin was drilled out by hand from underground shafts during the 18th and 19th centuries, and work finally ceased in the early 20th century; Golden Dagger was the last working Dartmoor tin mine. At Point ⑦ you will see all sorts of evidence on the ground: there's a buddle, used to sort the crushed ore, Dinah's House, last occupied in the 1940s, and Stamp's wheelpit (minus its waterwheel), which was last used in 1916.

When you reach Two Barrows, rest for a moment by the old granite wall and enjoy the panorama to the east. The views all along the Hamel Down ridge are breathtaking, and from this particular point you can see (from left to right) Hayne Down, Hound Tor, Honeybag Tor, Chinkwell Tor, and the characteristic outline of Haytor. To the left again you can pick out where the hills drop towards the sea at Teignmouth. There is the most fantastic feeling of peace and freedom up here – it just has to be experienced.

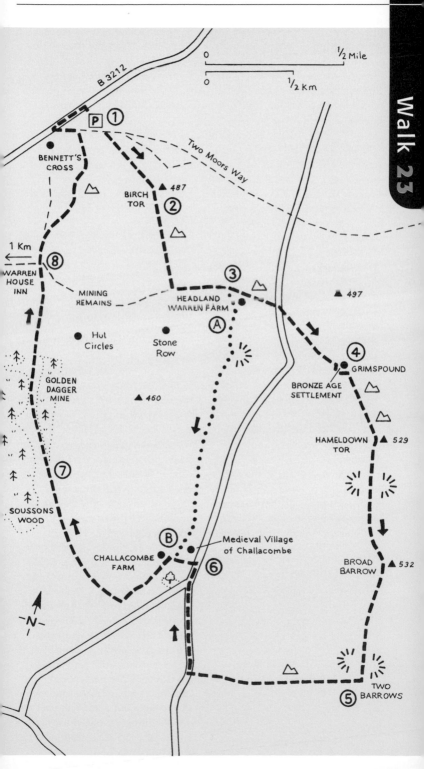

B 3212

0   ½ Mile
0   ½ Km

P ①

Two Moors Way

BENNETT'S
CROSS

BIRCH
TOR ② ▲ 487

1 Km

WARREN
HOUSE ⑧
INN

MINING
REMAINS

③

HEADLAND
WARREN FARM

▲ 497

Ⓐ

Hut
Circles

Stone
Row

④

GRIMSPOUND

BRONZE AGE
SETTLEMENT

GOLDEN
DAGGER
MINE

▲ 460

HAMELDOWN ▲ 529
TOR

⑦

SOUSSONS
WOOD

Ⓑ

Medieval Village
of Challacombe

CHALLACOMBE
FARM

⑥

BROAD
BARROW ▲ 532

-N-

⑤ TWO
BARROWS

W a l k   2 3

Walk 23 Directions

① Follow a narrow heathery path leading directly away from the car park towards **Birch Tor**, which can be seen on the horizon.

② A small path leads straight on from the tor downhill to meet a gritty track at right-angles. Turn left towards **Headland Warren Farm** in the valley ahead. Follow the path along a granite wall (right) to a wooden signpost.

③ Go straight on uphill to cross the road. Take the small path leading off right, up to **Grimspound**. Walk to the right and then through the 'entrance' in the perimeter wall.

④ At the centre of the enclosure turn right and climb steeply uphill to gain **Hameldown Tor** at 1,735ft (529m). The obvious path on the ridge top leads to **Broad Barrow** and then **Two Barrows**; where you reach a wall running ahead and downhill right.

⑤ Turn right to follow the wall down the valley side. The wall gives way to a line of small beech trees and there are superb views towards

Soussons Wood and the **Warren House Inn**. Cross the stock fence via a stile to join a permissive path, and over another stile onto the road. Turn right until you reach the drive to **Challacombe Farm**.

⑥ Turn left up the concrete drive. At the T-junction turn left to pass the farm and through a small gate. Keep right through the next gateway (signs to **Bennett's Cross**) and along the field edge.

⑥ The next gate/stile takes you into the edge of **Soussons Wood**. After a few paces you reach the fascinating remains of **Golden Dagger** tin mine where there's a detailed information board. It's worth having a good explore here. Follow the main track on. When it veers left continue ahead on a smaller bridleway signed to '**Bennett's Cross**' and proceed up the valley through a gate back onto low-lying yet open moorland, through masses of mining remains.

⑧ When you reach a junction of tracks either turn left over a stream, crossing by a ruined building and ascending to the **Warren House Inn**, or go straight on, keeping right where the path splits after a few paces. Follow the narrow and indistinct path uphill to a grassy gully. Climb out at the top, turn left and then right up to **Bennett's Cross** car park. Walk right up the road to your car.

Challacombe Valley

Another way to see Grimspound – but avoiding the Hamel Down ridge.
See map and information panel for Walk 23

•DISTANCE•	4¼ miles (7km)
•MINIMUM TIME•	2hrs 30min
•ASCENT / GRADIENT•	328ft (100m) ▲▲▲
•LEVEL OF DIFFICULTY•	🚶 🚶 🚶

Walk 24 Directions (Walk 23 option)

If you don't feel like walking up to Grimspound itself, but consider you can see it well enough from the lower levels, this alternative route cuts out the climb to **Hameldown Tor** and the walk along **Hamel Down** to **Two Barrows**.

At Point ③, turn right at the signpost following the bridleway signs for **Challacombe Farm**. Pass through a small gate in front of **Headland Warren farmhouse** and stables, to join the drive. At Point Ⓐ bear right to leave the drive through a gate and along the grassy undulating path along the bottom of the valley, keeping the wire fence left. When the cottages before **Challacombe Farm** come into view there seem to be two grassy ways ahead; keep to the higher one (right), keeping the old bank and wall remains right, to pass through a gate and in front of the cottages (Point Ⓑ).

The next gate joins the concrete drive to **Challacombe Farm** at the T-junction at Point ⑥. All along this shortcut you have great views of the Bronze Age settlement at

Grimspound, which dates from around 1300 BC. The climatic conditions on the moor then were quite different from today, and much of the moor was forested. Neolithic peoples began to clear areas of the moor, and the Bronze Age settlers continued the process.

The original enclosure wall (or, possibly, a double wall) was up to 6ft (1.8m) high and about 10ft (3m) wide, surrounding an area of about 4 acres (1.6ha), with two dozen hut circles inside. It was probably used for keeping stock safe, and would have been a pleasant place to live, situated on the slopes by the Grimslake stream, with good grazing.

It is thought by many to be Dartmoor's finest prehistoric monument. The site was extensively examined and partly reconstructed (and its significance fully realised), by the Dartmoor Exploration Committee in 1894.

WHERE TO EAT AND DRINK ⓘ
The **Warren House Inn** is the third highest inn in England, at 1,400ft (427m) above sea level. There's a fire that hasn't gone out since 1845, and the food is great. It is visible for many miles around, particularly from the south, and is a welcome sight for walkers.

Walk 25

Along the Dart Valley Way

From historic Totnes to the estate village of Ashprington via Sharpham.

•DISTANCE•	6 miles (9.7km)
•MINIMUM TIME•	2hrs 30min
•ASCENT / GRADIENT•	328ft (100m) ▲▲ ▲ ▲
•LEVEL OF DIFFICULTY•	🚶 🚶 🚶
•PATHS•	Easy field paths and country lanes, 14 stiles
•LANDSCAPE•	Fields and woodland on gentle slopes
•SUGGESTED MAP•	aqua3 OS Outdoor Leisure 20 South Devon
•START / FINISH•	Grid reference: SX 806603
•DOG FRIENDLINESS•	Dogs should be kept under control at all times
•PARKING•	Long stay car park at Steamer Quay
•PUBLIC TOILETS•	Opposite Steamer Quay

Walk 25 Directions

Once through **Baltic Wharf**, early on in the walk, look back at **Totnes**. You get a great view of the impressive Norman motte-and-bailey castle, and the 15th-century red sandstone church just down the High Street. The castle dominates the town, and from the motte you get a clear impression of the structure of the town, the original parts of which were walled in the 12th century. Much of the town walls remain today. There is evidence that there was a Saxon *burh* at Totnes in the 10th century, when coins were minted here. The town celebrates its heritage in many ways, including an Elizabethan market (Tuesdays, May to September), very appropriate for a town that has so many 15th- and 16th-century buildings. Much of the town's centre, including the historic East Gate, was badly damaged by fire in September 1990, but the sympathetic reconstruction is very successful.

Start the walk by going back along the road, then left into **Seymour Road**. At the main road turn left opposite **Seymour Terrace** to cross the late Georgian bridge. At the small roundabout turn left to walk through **The Plains**, and straight on. Follow the public footpath sign left along the edge of the river (pretty at high tide, muddy at low) to rejoin the road in front of the **Steam Packet Inn**. Go left past the pub and across the road, then up the ramp to pass through open

---

WHERE TO EAT AND DRINK ⓘ

Totnes has a huge range of cafés and eating places – largely wholefood and many organic – you're spoilt for choice. On the walk you pass the café on Steam Quay, and the **Steam Packet Inn**, which enjoys a good position by the river and offers a wide range of food, and accommodation. It's a free house, and families are welcome. The **Durant Arms** in the middle of Ashprington has been an inn since 1725, and is also advertised as a hotel and restaurant. It's a very pretty building, and was renamed in honour of the local Durant family from nearby Sharpham.

metal gates into **Baltic Wharf**; the footpath is signed here 'Dart Valley Way'. At the metal fence at the end of the compound the path turns right up steps and over a stile, then leads between wire fences above the **Goss Challenges** boatyard.

WHILE YOU'RE THERE

It's worth having a better look at **Totnes Castle**, one of the most complete surviving examples of a Norman motte-and-bailey construction in Britain. Built near the north gate of the town, the late 11th-century motte rises 55ft (16.8m) from the bailey, and from its substantial 12th-century walls you can get a clear picture of the historic development of the town below you, aided by English Heritage's effective artwork reconstructions. The castle was built in the heart of the Saxon town, and the great surrounding ditch, part of the original fortification, is today filled with cottages and gardens.

The path passes through a kissing gate, leads into mixed woodland, and down steps towards the river. The next gate leads into a meadow; keep straight on along the bottom to cross the next stile into a small copse. You're likely to see one of the popular river cruisers across the saltmarshes (left), en route for Dartmouth, a pleasant 1¼ hour trip downriver.

Pass over a small stile and wooden walkway by a little disused quarry, then up wooden steps and over a stile into a field. The next stile leads through a small plantation, then through a five-bar gate into a broad, undulating field with parkland trees. The path runs along the bottom edge and curves right, with views over the saltmarshes. A battered gate leads to an earthy path; a second gate leads to a farm track running through organic crop fields (the Sharpham Estate). **Sharpham House** was built between 1770 and 1824 for Captain Philemon Pownall, with prize money from the capture of a Spanish treasure ship, and the estate is now a working vineyard, situated on the warm south-facing slopes above the Dart.

When the path ahead is barred (private), pass through a metal gate then immediately right over a stile. Walk steeply uphill to enter a deciduous wood over a stile, then left along the edge of a larch plantation. This long, easy path gives way to a pretty wooded track (**Leafy Lane**), to meet the tarmac lane by the entrance to **Sharpham Vineyard & Creamery**. Go straight ahead along the lane to drop down into Ashprington village by the **Durant Arms** (left).

Ashprington is very quiet and well preserved, tucked away in a fold of the hills. It was recorded in the Domesday Book as the Manor of Aisbertona, and until an auction in September 1940 most of the greystone houses, with characteristic latticed windows and bargeboarded gables, belonged to the Sharpham Estate. **St David's Church**, passed on your way into the village, dates from the 12th century. To get back to Totnes simply retrace your steps.

Wartime Secrets at Inner Froward Point

The delights of Coleton Fishacre – and a surprise on the cliffs near Kingswear.

•DISTANCE•	4½ miles (7.2km)
•MINIMUM TIME•	3hrs
•ASCENT / GRADIENT•	525ft (160m) ▲▲▲
•LEVEL OF DIFFICULTY•	🚶🚶 🚶🚶 🚶🚶
•PATHS•	Varying coast path, tracks and lanes, steep steps, 9 stiles
•LANDSCAPE•	Coastal cliff top and deep combes
•SUGGESTED MAP•	aqua3 OS Outdoor Leisure 20 South Devon
•START / FINISH•	Grid reference: SX 910513
•DOG FRIENDLINESS•	Dogs should be kept under control at all times
•PARKING•	National Trust car park at Coleton Camp
•PUBLIC TOILETS•	None on route

BACKGROUND TO THE WALK

This is a walk that's full of surprises. Starting near the lovely National Trust house and gardens at Coleton Fishacre, it runs along a particularly beautiful piece of the South West Coast Path (much of which was purchased by the National Trust in 1982), dropping down into Pudcombe Cove, and along the lower edge of the gardens, before climbing steeply up the other side of the valley and back onto the open cliff. And it's here that the surprises start – first of all you are quite likely to encounter a group of Shetland ponies, seemingly rather out of place on the South Devon coast, but allowed to graze freely to encourage regeneration of the indigenous vegetation. Further on along the path you will find all sorts of strange concrete structures scattered about the cliffs, causing you to wonder what on earth it is you've stumbled across. The scenery changes again as the walk takes you inland along the eastern side of the Dart estuary, with fine views of the 15th-century Dartmouth and Kingswear castles. For sheer variety and constantly changing themes, this walk is very hard to beat!

An Arts and Crafts House

Given to the National Trust in 1982 by Roland Smith, Coleton Fishacre enjoys a spectacular setting in this very quiet corner of South Devon – it's very much off the beaten track. The house, reflecting the Arts and Crafts tradition, was designed and built in 1925–6 for Rupert and Lady Dorothy D'Oyley Carte, of Gilbert and Sullivan fame. It is sited at the head of a deep, sheltered combe, providing the perfect environment for its 15-acre (6ha) sub-tropical garden, based around a succession of streams and water features that fall gently down the narrow combe towards the sea at Pudcombe Cove.

The remains of Kingswear Castle (1491–1502) are passed after Point ⑥. Similar in shape to the square tower at Dartmouth Castle on the opposite shore, it was abandoned soon after 1643, outclassed by the range of guns available at its counterpart (▶ Walk 27), and today belongs to the Landmark Trust and is available as holiday accommodation. The official title of the group of buildings encountered on the coast path south of Kingswear is the Inner Froward Point Coast Defence Battery, dating from World War Two and almost complete, apart from the guns. There are the remains of all kinds of wartime constructions here, apart from the lookout just above the sea. The site includes the foundations of several Nissen huts, two shell magazines, two gun positions and a shell incline, and two searchlight emplacements near sea level. It's all a trifle unexpected after the peaceful approach along the coast path but reflects the importance of the river mouth to successive military generations.

Walk 26 Directions

① When you enter the car park turn right and park along the right edge. Walk through the kissing gate in the top right corner to take the National Trust's permissive path towards a metal gate and stile ('**National Trust Coleton Barton Farm**'). Go along the field edge and over the stile down to another stile at the bottom of the field, then left diagonally to another stile. Walk uphill to reach the coast path (signs to **Pudcombe Cove** right).

② Turn right and follow the path along the cliff. Climb over a stile and walk steeply downhill and over a footbridge to reach the gate at the bottom of **Coleton Fishacre** gardens (there is no public right of way into the gardens here).

Walk 26

③ Turn left, following coast path signs, to pass steps to the cove and very steeply up wooden steps to leave the estate over a stile and onto **Coleton Cliffs**. At the next stile the path drops steeply, then climbs again above **Old Mill Bay** – with great views of the **Mew Stone** – followed by a steep climb up to **Outer Froward Point**, with views towards Start Point. The path undulates, then climbs steeply to reach the back of **Froward Cove**.

WHILE YOU'RE THERE ℹ

Take a ride on the **Paignton and Kingswear Steam Railway**. The station is near the lower ferry slipway in Kingswear. Constructed in 1864, the route passes along the wooded east bank of the Dart, then over the Greenway Viaduct, through Greenway Tunnel, back to the coast at Goodrington Sands and on to Paignton. You can link your trip with a cruise along the Dart, too, to enjoy an exploration of this beautiful landscape without muddying your boots.

---

④ Turn left, following signs for **Kingswear and Brownstone car park**. Cross one stile, walk steeply uphill, then cross another stile. Take the next coast path sign left, very steeply downhill through a wooded section. The path then undulates up and down towards the sea.

⑤ The look-out at **Inner Froward Point** is the next landmark, followed by 104 concrete steps up the cliff. Follow the tramway uphill and keep to the concrete walkway and steps to pass through some disused wartime buildings. At the top there is a junction of paths and a wooden footpath sign.

⑥ Turn left for **Kingswear** to walk through woodland behind **Newfoundland Cove**, over a stile and down a broad woodland track (with the estuary left). Plod down 84 steps to **Mill Bay Cove** and turn right down a tarmac way. Turn left over a stile and climb the 89 steps up to a lane, then 63 more steps to another lane.

⑦ Turn right (signed '**Brownstone**'). After 250yds (229m) the lane forks; gratefully take the right fork downhill (signed '**Access only to The Grange**') to **Home Cottage**.

⑧ Follow the footpath signs right up a steep, rocky path to a concrete lane, and on to pass **Higher Brownstone Farm**. Walk on up the lane to pass the National Trust car park, then the gates to **Coleton Fishacre**, and back to **Coleton Camp** car park.

WHERE TO EAT AND DRINK ℹ

This is a bit of a problem – there are no pubs in the immediate vicinity, and parking in Kingswear is difficult. If you do find a space, there is the **Royal Dart Hotel** by the ferry slipway, with good views over the river; the **Ship Inn**, next to the church, and the **Steam Packet Inn** on the road down to the ferry. There is also a **National Trust café** and restaurant at Coleton Fishacre.

WHAT TO LOOK FOR ℹ

The Tower (day beacon), set at 475ft (145m) above sea level above Inner and Outer Froward Point, can be seen for many miles. Hollow and built of stone in 1864, it stands 80ft (24m) high. Day beacons, or day marks, are unlit navigational aids, intended to assist those at sea during daylight hours. A path runs towards it from the wooden signpost at Point ⑤ of the walk, and then on to Brownstone, which you could use to shorten the walk by about ¾ mile (1.2km) – but you'd miss some superb scenery.

The Busy Port of Dartmouth and a Spectacular Castle

An easy round along the cliffs to Blackstone Point and Dartmouth Castle – and a ferry ride to the pub.

•DISTANCE•	3 miles (4.8km)
•MINIMUM TIME•	2hrs
•ASCENT / GRADIENT•	115ft (35m) ▲▲▲
•LEVEL OF DIFFICULTY•	🚶 🚶 🚶
•PATHS•	Easy coastal footpath and green lanes
•LANDSCAPE•	Farmland, cliff tops and river estuary
•SUGGESTED MAP•	aqua3 OS Outdoor Leisure 20 South Devon
•START / FINISH•	Grid reference: SX 874491
•DOG FRIENDLINESS•	Possibility of livestock in some fields
•PARKING•	National Trust car parks at Little Dartmouth
•PUBLIC TOILETS•	Dartmouth Castle

BACKGROUND TO THE WALK

Dartmouth seems to have everything. The town has a rich and illustrious history and, with its smaller sister Kingswear on the opposite shore, occupies a commanding position on the banks of the Dart. With its sheltered, deep-water harbour it developed as a thriving port and shipbuilding town from the 12th century. By the 14th century it enjoyed a flourishing wine trade, and benefited from the profits of piracy for generations. Thomas Newcomen, who produced the first industrial steam engine, was born here in 1663. Today pleasure craft and the tourist industry have taken over in a big way – the annual Royal Regatta has been a major event for over 150 years – but Dartmouth has lost none of its charm. One of its attractions is that there are all sorts of ways of getting there: by bus, using the town's park-and-ride scheme, by river, on a steamer from Totnes, by sea, on a coastal trip from Torbay, by steam train, from Paignton or, of course, on foot along the coast path.

Fortified River Mouth

Now cared for by English Heritage, 15th-century Dartmouth Castle enjoys an exceptionally beautiful position at the mouth of the Dart. Replacing the 1388 *fortalice* of John Hawley, it was one of the most advanced fortresses of the day and, with Kingswear Castle opposite (of which only the tower remains) was built to protect the homes and warehouses of the town's wealthy merchants. A chain was slung across the river mouth between the two fortifications, and guns fired from ports in the castle walls. Visitors can experience a representation of life in the later Victorian gun battery that was established. A record of 1192 infers that there was a monastic foundation on the site, leading to the establishment of St Petrock's Church, rebuilt in Gothic style within the castle precincts in 1641–2.

The cobbled quayside at Bayard's Cove, with its attractive and prosperous 17th- and 18th-century buildings (including the Customs House from 1739) was used during filming of the BBC TV series *The Onedin Line* in the 1970s. The wooded estuary a little upriver was also used for a scene supposedly set in 18th-century China, but filming was unwittingly thwarted by the sound of a steam train chuffing through the trees! The single-storey artillery fort at Bayard's Cove was built before 1534 to protect the harbour. You can still see the gunports at ground level and the remains of a stairway leading to a walled walk above. A plaque commemorates the sailing of the *Mayflower* and *Speedwell* from the quay in 1620.

Walk 27 **Directions**

① The car parks at **Little Dartmouth** are signposted off the B3205 (from the A379 Dartmouth-to-Stoke Fleming road). Go through the right-hand car park, following the signs 'Coast Path Dartmouth'. Continue through a kissing gate, keeping the hedge to your right. Walk through the next field, then through a kissing gate to join the coast path.

② Turn left; there are lovely views here west to **Start Point** and east towards the **Day Beacon** above **Kingswear**. The coast path runs a little inland from the cliff edge, but you can always go straight ahead to walk above **Warren Point** (a plaque reveals that the Devon Federation of Women's Institutes gave this land to the National Trust in 1970).

③ Continue left to pass above **Western Combe Cove** (with steps down to the sea) and then **Combe**

Point (take care – it's a long drop to the sea from here).

④ Rejoin the coast path through an open gateway in a wall and follow it above **Shinglehill Cove**. The path turns inland, passes through a gate, becomes narrow and a little overgrown, and twists along the back of **Willow Cove**. It passes through a wooded section (with a field on the left) and then climbs around the back of **Compass Cove**. Keep going to pass through a gate. Keep left to reach a wooden footpath post, then turn sharp right, down the valley to the cliff edge. Follow the path on, through a gate near **Blackstone Point**.

⑤ Leave the path right to clamber down onto the rocks here – you get a superb view over the mouth of the estuary. Retrace your steps and continue on the coast path as it turns inland along the side of the estuary and runs through deciduous woodland.

WHAT TO LOOK FOR ⓘ

Dartmouth, both on shore and on the water, is always buzzing with activity – it never stops. There's masses to watch including pleasure steamers, private cruisers, brightly-coloured dinghies, rowing boats, ferries, expensive ocean-going yachts, canoeists and even huge cruise ships, calling in for a night en route for sunnier climes. You'll also notice naval craft, ranging from old-fashioned whalers to modern frigates, and connected with the **Britannia Royal Naval College**, which overlooks the town. Princes Charles and Andrew both studied here. You may also hear the whistle of a steam train on the **Paignton-to-Kingswear railway**, which runs along the eastern side of the river to terminate at Kingswear Station.

WHILE YOU'RE THERE ⓘ

Catch the ferry from Stumpy Steps (just upriver from the castle), which within a few minutes will deposit you right in the centre of Dartmouth. You get a fabulous view of all those superb waterside residences that are tantalisingly difficult – if not impossible – to see from the lane above, and the ferry saves you a further mile (1.6km) walk. There's a continuous shuttle service from the castle from 10:15AM until 5PM.

---

⑥ The path meets a surfaced lane opposite **Compass Cottage**; go right onto the lane and immediately right again steeply downhill, keeping the wall to your left. At the turning space go right down steps to reach the castle and café.

⑦ Retrace your route up the steps to the tarmac lane at Point ⑥, then left to pass **Compass Cottage**, and straight on up the steep lane (signposted '**Little Dartmouth**') and through a kissing gate onto National Trust land.

⑧ The path runs along the top of a field and through a five-bar gate onto a green lane. Go through a gate and the farmyard at **Little Dartmouth** and ahead on a tarmac lane to the car park.

WHERE TO EAT AND DRINK ⓘ

There's the **Castle Tearooms** at Dartmouth Castle and, if you hop on the ferry, masses of very good eating places in Dartmouth – including the best takeaway prawn sandwiches ever, available from a shop on the right just past the lower ferry slipway. The **Royal Castle Hotel** overlooking the Boat Float in the middle of the town is a freehouse, with good food, as is the **Dartmouth Arms** at historic Bayard's Cove.

The Deep South at Prawle Point

This is a land of shipwrecks and smugglers, gannets and skuas, and some of the oldest rocks in Devon.

•DISTANCE•	4 miles (6.4km)
•MINIMUM TIME•	2hrs
•ASCENT / GRADIENT•	394ft (120m) ▲▲▲
•LEVEL OF DIFFICULTY•	🚶🚶 🚶🚶 🚶
•PATHS•	Green lanes, fields and coast path, rocky in places, 3 stiles
•LANDSCAPE•	Coastal farmland, rocky coves and level raised beaches
•SUGGESTED MAP•	aqua3 OS Outdoor Leisure 20 South Devon
•START / FINISH•	Grid reference: SX 781365
•DOG FRIENDLINESS•	Dogs to be kept under control at all times
•PARKING•	Around green in East Prawle (honesty box contributions)
•PUBLIC TOILETS•	By green in East Prawle

BACKGROUND TO THE WALK

It takes forever to get to East Prawle. The first signpost for the village, seen on the road not far from Chillington, between Torcross and Kingsbridge in the South Hams, tells you that it's only 4 miles (6.4km) away, but from then on you seem to be constantly turning left or right, along miles of typical banked, flower-filled Devon lanes, and never really getting very far. But then suddenly you're there – by the little green in the middle of the village, with its wonderfully remote yet open feeling. It's completely unspoilt, and very popular with Devon people who want a simple camping holiday without leaving the county. A week under canvas in good weather at Prawle and it's hard to leave. Prawle Point, just below the village, is the most southerly point in Devon. The easiest way to get there is by car, but it's far more satisfying to submit to the sleepy atmosphere and wander down the lanes and along the coast, past some of the most beautiful – and relatively undiscovered – coves in Devon.

Lookout Point
The lookout at Prawle Point is today manned on a voluntary basis to keep an eye on this particularly busy part of the coast. Originally a coastguard station, with a 270-degree field of vision, it was used by Lloyds of London to report the arrival of ships from across the Atlantic. In use as a naval signal service station from 1937 to 1940, it shut down as a permanent coastguard station in 1994. Prawle means 'lookout hill', so this practice could date back to Saxon times.

Prawle Point is home to a great variety of birds and, due to its southerly position, is visited by a wealth of early and rare varieties on spring and autumn migrations. Birdwatchers can usually see a full range of gulls, kestrels, cormorants, common terns, skylarks and common buzzards as well as gannets and great skuas (this is an internationally important habitat for these two species). The rare and localised cirl bunting is also a resident here – there were only 80 pairs in the country in 1989, but successful conservation measures has seen that risen to 450.

Devon's Oldest Rocks

The volcanic rocks of the coast here are some of Devon's oldest, dating back over 400 million years. Pressure from the earth's movements split the strata and realigned them into parallel bands. The pounding sea then created the split, angular rocks evident today. The raised beach below East Prawle, a distinctive platform 15ft (4.5m) above the present beach, was formed during the last two million years in times of warmer weather conditions and higher sea levels, which altered coastal erosion patterns.

Walk 28

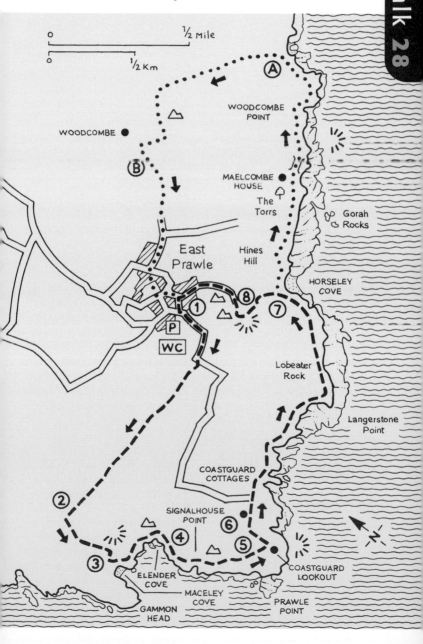

Walk 28 Directions

① Walk down the lane towards the sea, leaving the green to the left and a phone box right and following a footpath signed '**Prawle Point**'. After a few minutes the lane turns sharp left; go straight ahead along a deeply rutted level green lane marked '**Public Bridleway Gammon Head**'.

② The green lane ends at a T-junction (metal gate opposite); turn left down a very narrow grassy path between tumbledown, overgrown old walls. There are fine views of the coast ahead. Follow the path to the footpath post.

③ Turn right and immediately downhill to reach the coast path high above secluded **Maceley Cove**, with **Gammon Head** right. Turn left and walk along the path above **Elender Cove**. There is steep, scrambly access to both beaches but take care.

④ The path leads through a kissing gate and scrambles on around **Signalhouse Point**. A steep ascent is rewarded with fine views ahead to the wreck of the *Demetrios* on the rocks, with **Prawle Point** beyond. Follow the footpath posts through a kissing gate and across the grassy down, keeping to the right of the coastguard lookout ahead.

WHERE TO EAT AND DRINK ⓘ
East Prawle is blessed with two good pubs. The 18th-century **Freebooter Inn** is full of smuggling and shipwreck memorabilia. It's also very welcoming, and serves excellent food. The **Pig's Nose** has a menu geared towards families. You can also get snacks and refreshments at **Grunter's Café**.

⑤ At the coastguard lookout enjoy superb views east to **Lannacombe**, **Mattiscombe Sand** and **Start Point**. Take some time to explore the excellent visitor centre, which will tell you everything you want to know about the area. To continue, follow the grassy path inland towards the old coastguard cottages.

WHAT TO LOOK FOR ⓘ
The wreck of the *Demetrios*, a 700-tonne cargo ship that foundered on the rocks 300ft (92m) below the lookout at Prawle Point in December 1992 en route for a Turkish scrapyard, is evidence of just how tricky navigation is in these parts. There are 800 recorded shipwrecks along the South Devon coast, nine of which are around Prawle, including a Bronze Age wreck at Gammon Head, dating from around 1000 BC.

⑥ Turn right through a gate to pass in front of the cottages and along the edge of the level, grassy wavecut platform which lies just below the original Pleistocene cliffs here. Pass through a kissing gate and along lovely level meadows above low cliffs. Go through the next kissing gate, past the next footpath post and straight over an ivy-covered stile. Pass around the edge of the next field; **Maelcombe House** is now in sight ahead.

⑦ Follow the path as it turns inland and, soon after, cross a stone wall. Turn immediately left up the edge of the field. At the end of the hedge go left up the track.

⑧ Take the first stile right to go very steeply up the field. There are wonderful views back to the coast when you stop for a breather. Cross the stone stile at the top and continue right up the narrow rocky track to join the lane, ascending right steeply back to the village.

An East Prawle Extension

Round craggy Woodcombe Point towards Start Point – a tempting little extra.
See map and information panel for Walk 28

•**DISTANCE**•	6 miles (9.7km)
•**MINIMUM TIME**•	3hrs 20min
•**ASCENT / GRADIENT**•	590ft (180m) ▲▲▲
•**LEVEL OF DIFFICULTY**•	🚶🚶 🚶🚶 🚶

Walk 29 Directions (Walk 28 option)

If you can't drag yourself away from the coast path below **East Prawle**, here's an easy circular extension which only adds about 1¼ hours.

When you reach the stone wall at Point ⑦, keep straight on along the coast path. When you meet the track turn right to look at **Horseley Cove**. If you don't want to do that, keep going left and then right, signed 'Lannacombe'. A wooden stile leads into the level grounds of **Maelcombe House**. Two more stiles and a footbridge later, pass through a gate to leave the grounds. The coast path is now rocky and undulating. The path passes through a gate, then winds around the cliffs below **Woodcombe Point** (look out for kestrels) to reach great views towards **Lannacombe Bay**.

The path follows the line of the coast inland and passes through a gate, then through another gate. At Point Ⓐ the coast path goes straight on; turn left up a wooded, rocky public footpath (muddy in winter) to **Woodcombe**. This rises steeply to reach another gate, leading into a green lane.

Follow public bridleway signs where the lane veers left to join a farm track between fields.

At Point Ⓑ follow the bridleway ('**East Prawle**') left through a gate. Keep straight on (not down the green lane right) along the edge of the field, keeping the hedge right. At the end of the field the path cuts down right through a small gate into a copse, then runs uphill to join a green lane. This joins a tarmac lane; go straight on (signs left to **Maelcombe House**). At the next junction by the phone box go left and immediately right following public footpath signs to weave along a narrow path between the cottages. When you reach the lane turn left and then right to the village green.

WHAT TO LOOK FOR ⓘ

Keep an eye out for grey (or Atlantic) seals as you wend your away along the coast path. Although it's always exciting to catch sight of one of these wonderfully appealing creatures lounging on the rocks, and feels like a rare treat, there are actually about 85,000 grey seals around Britain (60 per cent of the world population). Naturally curious, they will watch you just as closely as you watch them, if they get the chance. A big bull seal can grow up to 7ft (2.1m) long, and can easily be recognised by his thick, heavy muzzle.

Walk 30

The Terrifying Sea Along the Coast to Start Point

The sea has left a sobering reminder of its strength on the coast from Slapton Ley to Start Point.

•DISTANCE•	6 miles (9.7km)
•MINIMUM TIME•	3hrs
•ASCENT / GRADIENT•	328ft (100m) ▲▲▲
•LEVEL OF DIFFICULTY•	🚶🚶 🚶 🚶
•PATHS•	Good coast path, 1 stile
•LANDSCAPE•	Undulating cliffs and shingle beaches
•SUGGESTED MAP•	aqua3 OS Outdoor Leisure 20 South Devon
•START / FINISH•	Grid reference: SX 823420
•DOG FRIENDLINESS•	Dogs to be kept under control at all times
•PARKING•	Long stay car park at Torcross
•PUBLIC TOILETS•	In Torcross, and by beach at North Hallsands

Walk 30 Directions

Visit the little village of **Torcross**, at the southern end of **Slapton Ley**, south of Dartmouth, on a sunny summer's day and it's quite impossible to believe that it could ever be anything but warm, calm and tranquil. The views south to **Start Point** are particularly wonderful in May, when the point shimmers under a carpet of bluebells. But on 16 January 1917 the fishing village of **Hallsands** just to the south was almost totally destroyed during a huge storm which smashed through the sea walls and washed the cottages away. Perhaps it was the result of extensive dredging work off the coast here between 1897 and 1902, when tons of shingle were removed for Royal Navy building work at Devonport in Plymouth. Around 1,600 tons were dredged up each day, so altering the patterns of coastal erosion. The remaining

villages still suffer – Torcross sea front was badly damaged during heavy storms in 1951 and 1979.

This is a versatile walk, giving a good feel for the coastline. You can turn back at **Beesands**, or **Hallsands**, or go all the way to the lighthouse at **Start Point**. From the blocked-off path to ruined Hallsands village, you can still see

---

WHAT TO LOOK FOR ⓘ

You'll notice an American **Sherman tank** in the car park, which was lost during the D-Day landing practices in 1944, and recovered from the sea in 1984. It now stands as a memorial to those American servicemen who perished during Operation Tiger, a training exercise that went tragically wrong in the early hours of 28 April 1944. Nine German torpedo boats intercepted a 3-mile (4.8km) long convoy of US vessels moving from Portland to Slapton Sands during a landing rehearsal. Two landing craft were destroyed, and two more damaged, leading to the loss of almost 1,000 lives.

Walk 30

the remains of some of the cottages. You glimpse the ruins from various points along the coast path, too.

Follow the footpath sign over the road to turn right along the concrete promenade (a sea defence scheme from 1980). At the end ascend steep steps onto a gritty track, following coast path signs, with great views back along **Slapton Ley**. This, the largest natural lake in the West Country, is a haven for goldeneye, grey herons, mute swans, tufted ducks, pochards, great crested grebes, mallards, moorhens and coots, and is popular with birdwatchers. There's a good information board by the **Duckery** near the car park.

Go through a gate into a field on the cliff top, then through the next gate and along a track which drops down with spectacular views over **Widdicombe Ley** and **Beesands**. The track runs behind the beach into the village, which has a slightly forgotten feel about it. Pass the tiny **St Andrew's Church** and the **Cricket Inn** (on the right), and continue straight on, following signs for **Hallsands**. Follow the path as it climbs steeply up the cliff and

on through a brackeny area. When **North Hallsands** comes into view, look carefully down to sea level to the ruined village beyond.

Go through the next gate and along the lower edge of the field. The beach at **North Hallsands** is quiet and remote, the houses across the field behind the beach were built to re-house some of the displaced villagers in 1924. Another gate leads into the next field; go through the next gate and field to reach the beach. Cross the beach to join the lane leading to **Hallsands Hotel**, then follow the coast path 'Start Point' up steps behind the hotel. This leads on to Trout's holiday apartments above Hallsands, former home to the indomitable Trout sisters, survivors of the devastation of 1917. Walk down to the gate above the old path to the village and look down at the ruins; there's a real feeling of desolation here.

Continue to follow the coast path towards **Start Point**. A couple of old apple trees have been blown over the path to form arches, giving an idea of the strength of the winds here. The path leads up to a stile to join the car park for **Start Point** and **Great Mattisombe Sand**, and the gate to the lighthouse. There are spectacular views back to **South Hallsands** and all along the length of the coast.

Walk 31

Salubrious Salcombe and Sleepy East Portlemouth

Only a short ferry trip apart, the contrasts across the Kingsbridge Estuary could not be greater.

•DISTANCE•	4 miles (6.4km)
•MINIMUM TIME•	2hrs
•ASCENT / GRADIENT•	377ft (115m) ▲▲▲
•LEVEL OF DIFFICULTY•	🚶🚶 🚶🚶 🚶🚶
•PATHS•	Good coast path, field paths and tracks
•LANDSCAPE•	River estuary, rocky coast and coves, farmland
•SUGGESTED MAP•	aqua3 OS Outdoor Leisure 20 South Devon
•START / FINISH•	Grid reference: SX 746385
•DOG FRIENDLINESS•	Dogs to be kept under control at all times
•PARKING•	Near phone box in East Portlemouth or in small parking bay
•PUBLIC TOILETS•	At Mill Bay, passed on Points ③ and ⑦

BACKGROUND TO THE WALK

Salcombe is a delightful place. The only trouble with Salcombe is that hundreds of other people think so too, and during the holiday season the narrow streets are packed – and it's not somewhere that you want to be jostled and bothered by the crowds. So it's great to come to Salcombe out of season or, better still, to park away from the town and approach it from a different direction.

There's a wonderful walk in along the coast path around Bolt Head, to the west of the estuary; or you can follow this walk from the tiny hamlet of East Portlemouth, opposite the town, from where you get some of the best views in the area over the mass of small boats in the harbour, and the various creeks upriver towards Kingsbridge. Once the haunt of smugglers and pirates, today it has a civilised, prosperous, and, as a result of its sheltered position and deep blue waters, an almost Mediterranean feel. It's a much smaller and gentler place than Dartmouth (▶ Walk 27), and extremely popular with the sailing fraternity, with safe waters for novices (at high tide) further up the estuary. The estuary is a marvellous place for young families, too. At low tide there is a run of sandy beaches all along the East Portlemouth side, enabling those staying in Salcombe simply to hop on the ferry for a day on the beach. (**Note:** Many of these sandy coves are cut off at high tide, ie there is no access from the shore – take care.)

Overbecks
From Limebury Point you can see across the estuary to Overbecks, an elegant Edwardian house in a magnificent setting above South Sands. Otto Overbeck, who lived here from 1928 to 1937, left the house and its 6-acre (2.4ha) garden to the National Trust, and it's worth visiting for the garden alone: there is a fantastic collection of rare and sub-tropical plants here, thriving in the temperate conditions. The house is fun, too (there's masses to keep children occupied). Overbeck was a collector of all manners of things, many of which – shells, toys, model boats, local shipbuilding tools – are on display today.

An Interesting Past

East Portlemouth has a totally different feel to Salcombe. It is small, very quiet and unspoilt, and somewhat belies its rather difficult history. During the 19th century half the population was evicted by the absentee landlord, the Duke of Cleveland, as a result of their preference for fishing and wrecking over working the land. The 15th-century church is dedicated to St Winwalloe, a 5th-century Celtic saint, and a fascinating gravestone in the churchyard reveals the death by burning at the stake of a girl who poisoned her employer in 1782.

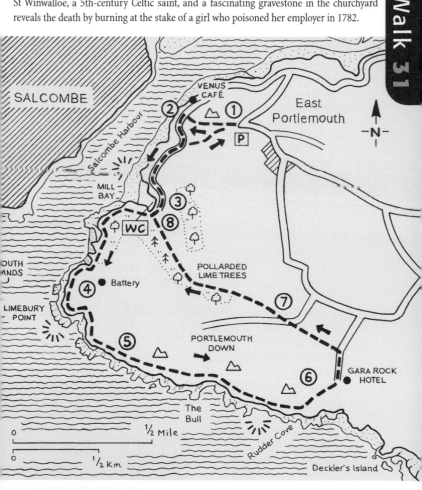

Walk 31 Directions

① Park on the verge near the phone box at **East Portlemouth** (or in the parking area – contributions to village hall fund). Walk through the parking area and steeply downhill on a narrow tarmac footpath signposted '**Salcombe**', which gives way to steep steps.

② When you reach the lane at the bottom of the steps, turn right if you want to visit the **Venus Café** and catch the ferry to Salcombe. If you want to get on with the walk, turn left along the lane as it follows the edge of the estuary. This is the official route of the coast path and it passes some very exclusive residences in almost sub-tropical surroundings.

③ The lane leads to the pretty, sandy beach at **Mill Bay**. Follow the coast path signs for **Gara Rock** along the edge of a sycamore wood, with lovely views across the estuary, and glimpses of inviting little coves.

④ At **Limebury Point** you reach open cliff, with great views to **South Sands** and **Overbecks** opposite and craggy **Bolt Head**. The coast path now veers eastwards below **Portlemouth Down**, which was divided into strip fields in the late 19th century.

> **WHILE YOU'RE THERE** ℹ️
> Catch the **ferry** to the other side and explore the pretty little town of Salcombe. The ferry runs every day, from 8AM–7PM on weekdays and from 8:30AM–7PM on weekends and bank holidays. There's also a lovely river trip by ferry from Salcombe to Kingsbridge.

⑤ The path along this stretch undulates steeply, and is rocky in places. Keep going until you reach the bench and viewpoint over the beach at **Rickham Sands**. Just beyond this, as the coast path continues right along the cliffs (there is reasonable access to the beach), take the left fork and climb steeply up below the lookout to reach the wall in front of **Gara Rock Hotel**.

⑥ Turn left to reach the hotel drive and walk straight on up the lane. After 100yds (91m) turn left through a gate in the hedge signposted '**Mill Bay**'. Walk straight across the field (the roped-off area indicates a car park for the beach) with lovely views to **Salcombe** and **Malborough church** beyond.

> **WHAT TO LOOK FOR** ℹ️
> Many stretches of the coast path are resplendent with wild flowers virtually all the year round, and during the summer months the path below Portlemouth Down is incredible. There are banks of purple wild thyme, heather, gorse, red campion, bladder campion, tiny yellow tormentil and pretty blue scabius. Look out too for the common dodder, a parasitic plant with pretty clusters of pink flowers. It draws the life out of its host plant, often heather or gorse, via suckers.

Go through a small copse, then a gate and across the farm track. Go through a metal gate down the public footpath.

⑦ This leads onto a beautiful bridle path, running gradually downhill beneath huge, ancient pollarded lime trees, with a grassy combe to the right. The path leads past the car park to reach **Mill Bay**.

⑧ Turn right along the lane. If you want to avoid the steps, look out for a footpath sign pointing right, up a narrow, steep, path to regain **East Portlemouth** and your car; if not, continue along the lane and retrace your steps up the steep tarmac path.

> **WHERE TO EAT AND DRINK** ℹ️
> Salcombe has a mass of pubs, cafés and restaurants, but if you want to stay on the East Portlemouth side try the **Venus Café**. It's in a glorious position by the ferry slipway, with a pretty garden looking across the water. The café serves great food and drink (try the *panini*), and is open every day from the end of March to the end of October unless the weather is absolutely dreadful. The **Gara Rock Hotel** (originally coastguard cottages) is open to non-residents.

Peace and Solitude in the Erme Estuary

A magical part of the county's south coast that even those who live in Devon seldom manage to find.

•DISTANCE•	5½ miles (9km)
•MINIMUM TIME•	2hrs 30min
•ASCENT / GRADIENT•	394ft (120m) ▲▲▲
•LEVEL OF DIFFICULTY•	👫 👫 👫
•PATHS•	Fields, tracks and good coast path, 7 stiles
•LANDSCAPE•	Rolling farmland, river estuary and cliff top
•SUGGESTED MAP•	aqua3 OS Outdoor Leisure 20 South Devon
•START / FINISH•	Grid reference: SX 635478
•DOG FRIENDLINESS•	Dogs to be kept under control at all times
•PARKING•	By the church in Kingston village
•PUBLIC TOILETS•	None on route

BACKGROUND TO THE WALK

This walk is centred on one of those places that very few people ever seem to find. It's almost as if Kingston and the lovely estuary of the River Erme are a jealously guarded secret by those 'in the know'. Both are rarely mentioned in the standard tourist literature. This part of the South Hams isn't really on the way to anywhere, and it's a fairly long trek along narrow, winding lanes to get there. But it's so worthwhile – you really feel as if you've stumbled on to somewhere secret, special and undiscovered.

The Flete Estate

The lands on the opposite side of the Erme are part of the Flete Estate, most famous these days for providing the setting for much of the filming of Ang Lee's adaptation of Jane Austen's *Sense and Sensibility* in the 1990s, starring Emma Thompson and Kate Winslet. Recorded in the Domesday Book, Flete was originally a Saxon estate. The later large Elizabethan manor house was incorporated into a neo-Elizabethan mansion in 1878 by Norman Shaw. Gothic-style restoration had already taken place in 1835, and the façade of the house dates to this time – it's an impressive, if slightly mixed up, building. The estate is not generally open to the public, and is now run as a home for the elderly. The house was lived in by the Heles in the 17th century, and there is an unusual monument with 22 tiered figures, representing three generations of the family, in the pretty church at Holbeton, which has a graceful early 14th-century tower and spire.

The River Erme

When you arrive at the Erme estuary it's hard to think that anything much has ever happened here. But the River Erme has a long and interesting history. It rises on Dartmoor, not far south of Nun's Cross (► Walk 36) and runs south to leave the moor at Harford, passing through an area of intensive Bronze Age occupation. There is evidence of hut circles, stone rows and cists and, in later medieval times, tin mining activity. Piles Copse in the upper Erme valley is one of the last three remaining areas of ancient oak woodland on the moor (▶ Walk 38). Further downstream there is evidence of lime kilns, and, before the estuary silted up, small vessels imported coal and limestone for burning. The only way to negotiate the ever-changing sand bars was to use a pilot, and the remains of his cottage can be seen at the back of Wonwell Beach today. The only way across the river is by wading, and the coast path signs on either side of the river indicate where it's possible to cross with care at low tide.

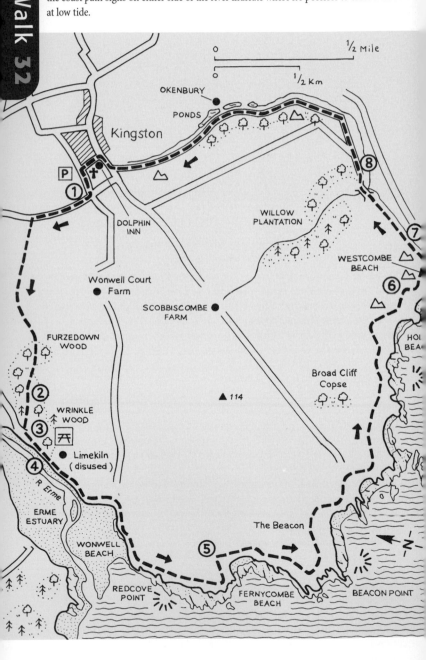

Walk 32 Directions

① With the church left, follow the lane uphill to **Wonwell Gate** and turn right down the lane signed '**Wonwell Beach**'. When it bends sharp left then right, turn left through a gate/stile and straight on, keeping the hedge left. Pass through the hedge into the next field, then follow the sign right, diagonally across the field to enter **Furzedown Wood** over a stile into a green lane.

② This leads into the next field; cross that, then go over a stile into **Wrinkle Wood** and follow the narrow path steeply downhill to meet a lane.

③ Turn left; there is limited parking for the beach here. Walk down to look at the **Erme estuary**, an attractive spot for a picnic.

WHERE TO EAT AND DRINK ⓘ
Kingston's 16th-century **Dolphin Inn** is quite something. There are pretty beer gardens, one with a play area, and good food. The next pub, 2 miles (3.2km) to the south east, is the **Journey's End** at Ringmore (▶ Walk 33).

④ Retrace your steps and follow the coast path signs up steps right signed '**Bigbury**'. Follow the narrow wooded path, which leads onto and along the back of **Wonwell Beach**. Go up a flight of steps, over a stile and straight on along the estuary to **Redcove Point** (with superb views to **Battisborough Island** opposite).

⑤ The path veers eastwards over a stile (National Trust **Scobbiscombe Farm**), then sweeps across a broad grassy area above **Fernycombe Beach** to reach **Beacon Point**, with glorious views opening up ahead.

Walk on through a small deep combe and up to a gate at the bench overlooking **Hoist Beach**, before the path drops down into a deep combe and climbs up through another gate.

WHILE YOU'RE THERE ⓘ
If the tide is low enough, wade across the river to **Mothecombe**. Its beautifully sandy beach is only open to the public Wednesday, Saturday and Sunday (all year), but in the village there's a tea room in the old school by the car park and toilets too.

⑥ Follow the steep and difficult (often slippery) descent to quiet **Westcombe Beach**. Take great care here, parts are stepped, but even the steps are sandy and it's easy to skid.

⑦ Turn left over a stile at the back of the beach, following signs for **Kingston** (this is a permissive path, unmarked on maps). The path has a wire fence left and stream right; walk over a wooden footbridge right to cross the stream and enter a willow plantation. The path twists out through a strip of woodland.

⑧ Cross over a stile and straight on up a pleasant, gradually ascending green lane (a bridleway to **Kingston**). Continue on to pass the ponds at **Okenbury** right (the track is muddy in places). The track runs into a tarmac lane, and back uphill into **Kingston**. Turn right, then left to the church and your car.

WHAT TO LOOK FOR ⓘ
First recorded in 1243, **Kingston** is a tucked-away village, a pleasure to explore. There's nothing exceptional, but its isolated yet cosy feel, and the flower-bedecked cottages, soothe away the pressures of modern life. The church dates mainly from the 14th century.

Burgh Island Paradise

A chance to mingle with the stars in an Art Deco dream and have a drink in Devon's oldest inn.

•DISTANCE•	3 miles (4.8km)
•MINIMUM TIME•	1hr 45min
•ASCENT / GRADIENT•	246ft (75m) ▲▲▲
•LEVEL OF DIFFICULTY•	秫 秫 秫
•PATHS•	Fields, tracks (muddy in winter) and coast path, 4 stiles
•LANDSCAPE•	Rolling coastal farmland and cliff top
•SUGGESTED MAP•	aqua3 OS Outdoor Leisure 20 South Devon
•START / FINISH•	Grid reference: SX 651442
•DOG FRIENDLINESS•	Dogs to be kept under control at all times
•PARKING•	Huge car park at Bigbury-on-Sea
•PUBLIC TOILETS•	At car park

BACKGROUND TO THE WALK

The broad, sandy beaches and dunes at Bigbury-on-Sea and Bantham, at the mouth of the River Avon south of Kingsbridge, attract hundreds of holidaymakers every summer, drawn by the appeal of sun, sand and sea. There's no doubt that this is a perfect spot for a family day out. Gone are the days of the 16th or 17th centuries when Bigbury was merely famous for its catches of pilchards! But there's something else appealing about this part of the South Devon coast. Just off Bigbury beach, 307yds (282m) from shore, lies craggy Burgh Island, with its famous hotel gazing at the mainland. This extraordinary island is completely surrounded by the sea at high tide but is accessible via the weird and wonderful sea tractor that ploughs its way through the waters.

The Enigma of Burgh Island

The island was known as *la Burgh* in the 15th century, and later Borough Island. There was a chapel dedicated to St Michael on its summit in 1411, and it has been likened to the much larger St Michael's Mount in Cornwall. The remains of a 'huer's hut' at the top of the island – a fisherman's lookout – is evidence of the times when pilchard fishing was a mainstay of life here too, hence the building of the Pilchard Inn, housed in one of the original fisherman's cottages. But it is the island's more recent history that is so fascinating. It was bought in 1929 by wealthy industrialist Archibald Nettlefold, who built the Burgh Island Hotel, much as we see it today. He ran it as a guest house for friends and celebrities, and it became a highly fashionable venue for the jet-set in the 1930s. Noel Coward was among the famous who visited, and it is thought that Edward, Prince of Wales and Wallis Simpson escaped from the limelight here; but the island's most famous connection has to be with Agatha Christie. Two of her books – *Evil Under the Sun* and *And Then There Were None* – were written here, and the influence of the hotel and its location on her writing is clear. By the mid 1980s the hotel had fallen into disrepair, and two London fashion consultants, Beatrice and Tony Porter, bought the island and restored the hotel to its original 1930s Art Deco glory, complete with the famous Palm Court and authentic Twenties cocktail bar. For a bit of escapism Burgh Island is hard to beat – but take your cheque book!

Walk 33

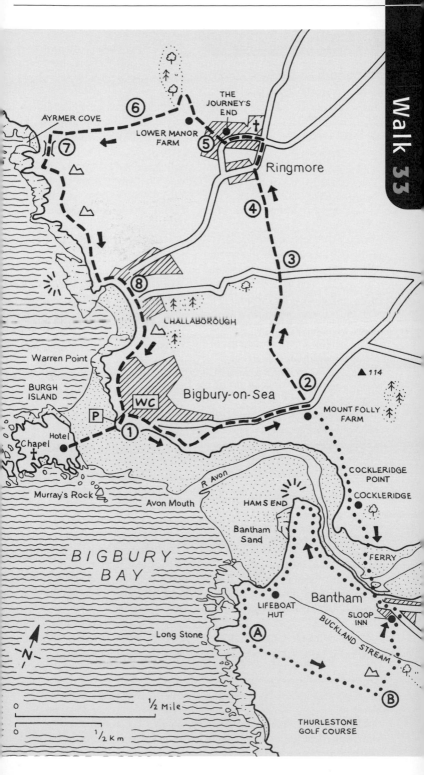

⑥ AYRMER COVE

⑦

THE JOURNEY'S END

LOWER MANOR FARM ⑤

Ringmore

④

③

⑧

CHALLABOROUGH

Warren Point

BURGH ISLAND

WC

P ① Bigbury-on-Sea

② MOUNT FOLLY FARM

Hotel

Chapel

Murray's Rock

R Avon

Avon Mouth

HAMS END

Bantham Sand

COCKLERIDGE POINT

COCKLERIDGE

FERRY

BIGBURY BAY

LIFEBOAT HUT

Bantham

SLOOP INN

BUCKLAND STREAM

Ⓐ

Long Stone

Ⓑ

THURLESTONE GOLF COURSE

N

½ Mile

½ Km

▲ 114

Walk 33

Walk 33 **Directions**

① Leave the car park through the entrance. Follow coast path signs right, (for the low tide route to the seasonal ferry to Bantham ► Walk 34), then left towards the road, then left again up a grassy area. Turn left before the bungalow, then left (unmarked path) to reach the road. Turn right and walk steeply uphill to **Mount Folly Farm**.

② Turn left along a gravelly track (signed '**Ringmore**'). At the top of the field is a junction of paths; go through the gate left, then through the metal gate ahead, keeping downhill. Cross a stile and walk downhill through a kissing gate. Cross the farm track and up the field, to reach a high stile, then descend steps into a narrow lane.

WHERE TO EAT AND DRINK ⓘ

The wonderful **Bay Café** at Bigbury has great views over Burgh Island. There's a **Venus Café** (► Walk 31), and a beach café at Challaborough. The **Journey's End** at Ringmore is full of atmosphere and has great food. Don't expect to drop into the **Burgh Island Hotel** unless you've brought your cocktail dress or bow-tie with you – but you can always make do with the **Pilchard Inn**.

---

③ Cross over, following signs for **Ringmore**, through the left of the two gates. Walk down into the next combe, keeping the hedgebank right. Cross the stream at the bottom on a concrete walkway, and over a stile. Ignore the path left, but go straight ahead, uphill, through a plantation and gate onto a narrow path between a fence and hedge.

④ Pass through a kissing gate, then turn right through an open gateway. Turn immediately left uphill to a metal gate/stile to join a track that leads to **Ringmore**. Turn right at the lane, then left at the church to find the **Journey's End** on the right.

⑤ From the pub turn right down the narrow lane which gives way to a footpath. It winds round to meet a tarmac lane. Turn left downhill. Walk straight on down the track (signed to '**Lower Manor Farm**') and keep going down past the '**National Trust Ayrmer Cove**' notice. After a small gate the track splits; keep left (unsigned) and straight on.

WHILE YOU'RE THERE ⓘ

Take a ride on the lumbering sea tractor over to **Burgh Island**. It's great fun and saves getting your feet wet as the tide rushes in. The tractor, designed specifically for the purpose, runs all year round (every ½ hour in summer, every hour in winter; last tractor 11:30PM). It can operate in 10ft (3.5m) of seawater and in gale conditions up to force 9 – though I wouldn't like to try it!

---

⑥ Turn left through a kissing gate and walk towards the cove on a grassy path above the combe (left). Pass through a gate and over two stiles to gain the beach.

⑦ Follow coast path signs ('**Challaborough**') left over a small footbridge then climb very steeply uphill to the cliff top and great views over **Burgh Island**. The cliffs are crumbly here – take care. The path is narrow, with a wire fence left, and leads to **Challaborough** – basically one huge holiday camp.

⑧ Turn right along the beach road and follow the track that leads uphill along the coast towards **Bigbury**. Go straight on to meet the tarmac road, then right on a narrow gravel path to the car park.

An Excursion to Bantham

Get away from it all by catching the ferry to tranquil Bantham Quay.
See map and information panel for Walk 33

•DISTANCE•	2½ miles (4km)
•MINIMUM TIME•	1hr 30min
•ASCENT / GRADIENT•	262ft (80m) ▲▲ ▲ ▲
•LEVEL OF DIFFICULTY•	林林 林林 林林

Walk 34 Directions
(Walk 33 option)

If the whole Bigbury/Burgh Island experience is too much for you, here's an extension across the river to quieter Bantham. It also stands alone as a separate walk. Although the ferry times are limited, you can (in theory) hail the ferryman outside 'official hours'. Follow the route for Walk 33 to **Mount Folly Farm** (Point ①). Turn right, following coast path signs 'Cockleridge'. Cross a stile, and a field above the **Avon**, then another stile and carry on to the dunes of **Cockleridge Point**. Follow footpath posts to the ferry notice board (summer only, Monday–Saturday, 10AM–11AM, 3PM–4PM).

Cross the Avon to pretty **Bantham Quay** and boathouse. Follow the path uphill to the car park entrance. Turn right (coast path signs), keeping right of the white gate. Keep right where the sandy path splits and walk around the perimeter of **Hams End** for great views. Keep on to cross the dunes and along the back of the beach. Rejoin the coast path by the lifeboat hut. Turn left, then immediately right, following coast path signs

over a stile. **Note**: the cliff edge here is unstable – keep to the path. The path runs up the cliff and over a stile to a footpath post/notice board at Thurlestone golf course. At Point Ⓐ turn left inland, following the white posts, then an old wall on the left. At the end of the grassy area cross a stile and turn immediately left over another stile by a footpath post (Point Ⓑ). Cross another stile and go very steeply down into the combe, aiming for a footpath post. Go past this and right, then left over a stile. Cross **Buckland Stream** and follow the footpath sign to the left. At the footpath post turn right, over a stile and up a narrow path. Go round the next stile to find the 16th-century **Sloop Inn** (and the best summer pudding in Devon!) on the left. After your break turn left from the pub to pass a beautiful row of unspoilt thatched cottages, then right downhill to reach **Bantham Quay** and the ferry.

WHILE YOU'RE THERE ⓘ
Explore **Ringmore**, a pretty village, with a mass of thatched cottages dating from the 16th to 18th century. The Journey's End, an old smuggling inn, is one of the oldest buildings in Devon (c 1300), built to house the labourers working on the church. It's named after RC Sherriff's play, part of which was written here.

Walk 35

A Wilderness Picnic by the East Dart River

From Postbridge this is a relatively easy walk, taking you into the heart of the wilderness of Dartmoor.

•DISTANCE•	4 miles (6.4km)
•MINIMUM TIME•	2hrs
•ASCENT / GRADIENT•	360ft (110m)
•LEVEL OF DIFFICULTY•	
•PATHS•	Drift lane and narrow rocky or grassy paths, 2 stiles
•LANDSCAPE•	Flat-bottomed river valley and undulating open moorland
•SUGGESTED MAP•	aqua3 OS Outdoor Leisure 28 Dartmoor
•START / FINISH•	Grid reference: SX 646788
•DOG FRIENDLINESS•	Dogs can run free on moor, but should be under control
•PARKING•	Dartmoor National Park car park, Postbridge (honesty box)
•PUBLIC TOILETS•	At car park

Walk 35 Directions

Most visitors to Dartmoor will, at some point, drive right across the moor, and so can't fail to follow the old route via Postbridge. Situated at a natural stopping place half-way across the moor, there has been a ford and clapper bridge (now restored) over the East Dart River here for centuries. The first written reference to the bridge was in 1675, but it was probably built 300 years earlier. The banks of the river here are very popular with picnickers, but there's a much more attractive and quieter picnic spot just an hour's walk away upriver.

Postbridge developed after the Moretonhampstead to Tavistock toll road was constructed in the late 18th century. The toll house here is recorded as taking £100 per annum in the 1820s, whereas that at Princetown took only £20, emphasising Postbridge's

importance on the main route across Dartmoor. There was an inn, the Greyhound, here in the late 18th century, but that had turned into a farm by the end of the 19th century and the Temperance Inn (now the East Dart Hotel) was built to replace it. It's strange to think that originally no alcoholic drink was available here – a potential disaster for today's thirsty walkers!

WHERE TO EAT AND DRINK

The **Lydgate House Hotel** is signposted off the B3212 near the bridge and serves excellent cream teas. The **East Dart Hotel** is a free house with a good range of food and offering accommodation. There's a beer garden and families are welcome. There's also a post office and stores here, and a small petrol station.

Leave the car park by the information centre on the right, and follow the path through the bank. It veers right towards the open moor through a broad, marshy area – an old drift lane,

Walk 35

Moorland walks such as this are frequently accompanied by the warbling song of the **skylark** in late spring and summer. This attractive little brown bird (barely 7in/18cm) rises almost vertically and hovers several hundred feet above the ground, from where it will entertain you with its unmistakable song. Nesting in grassy tussocks at ground level, the skylark is actually Britain's most widely breeding species of bird.

used originally for driving livestock up from the farmland to summer pasture on the moor. Many are still used at the annual pony drifts each autumn, but this one has been blocked by early 20th-century newtake walls. The lane ends at a gate by a line of beech trees and a granite wall. Go through and follow the track uphill to run alongside a wire fence/wall on the right. Just below, towards the river, is the site of **Roundy Park**, a Bronze Age enclosure with a restored *kist* (grave), dating from around 4,000 years ago. There are lovely views over the river to **Hartland Tor**.

The footpath crosses two brooks (**Braddon Lake**) on easy stepping stones, then runs uphill to a stile in the wall ahead. Cross the stile and follow the path along the course of a disused, overgrown leat on the left, which you can see running

along the contours of the hill when you look back over the stile. The path turns north to run above the **East Dart River** as the valley becomes narrower, with glorious views downriver towards **Bellever Forest**.

A stile brings you closer to the river, and onto a level marshy area. At this point you really do feel as if you are in the heart of the wilderness. On the other side of the **East Dart** here, near where **Winney's Down Brook** joins, are the circular remains of a beehive hut. These were built by tinners as somewhere to hide their tools. Keep near to the river – you will soon find the leat again – and follow it as it bends round sharp left. At this point you will see deep pools of crystal-clear water, and a broad grassy area, just perfect for a picnic.

Walk on a little further upstream. The river rushes faster here, tumbling over rocks, and you meet a stile. You can go on further upstream if you wish, but the path becomes indistinct and difficult. Turn back at this point and take the path ahead (not by the river) that runs around the bottom of the hillslope right. This will bring you back to the next stile and the path home to **Postbridge**.

Princetown: Thomas Tyrwhitt's Dream

There was great industrial activity here in the late 18th and early 19th centuries, but it's still the middle of nowhere!

•DISTANCE•	7 miles (11.3km)
•MINIMUM TIME•	3hrs
•ASCENT / GRADIENT•	328ft (100m) ▲ ▲ ▲
•LEVEL OF DIFFICULTY•	🚶 🚶 🚶
•PATHS•	Tracks, leat-side paths and rough moorland
•LANDSCAPE•	Open moorland
•SUGGESTED MAP•	aqua3 OS Outdoor Leisure 28 Dartmoor
•START / FINISH•	Grid reference: SX 588735
•DOG FRIENDLINESS•	Can be off the lead at all times, but watch for sheep
•PARKING•	Main car park in Princetown (honesty box)
•PUBLIC TOILETS•	By car park

BACKGROUND TO THE WALK

Even on a summer's day, when fluffy clouds scud across a blue sky and the high moor looks particularly lovely, Princetown is bleak. There's nothing soft and gentle about the place – most of the buildings are functional in the extreme, uncompromising, grey and harsh. The town, 1,395ft (425m) above sea level, and with an average annual rainfall of 82in (2,160mm), was founded by Sir Thomas Tyrwhitt in the late 18th century, and named in honour of the Prince Regent, to whom he was both a friend and private secretary.

Dartmoor Prison

Tyrwhitt persuaded the government to build a prison here for French prisoners from the Napoleonic wars. Building work started in 1806, and the first prisoners were in situ by 1809, joined by Americans in 1813. At one time 7,000 men were held. Closed in 1813, the prison reopened in 1850 as a civilian establishment, which it remains to this day – a monumental building, best seen from the Two Bridges to Tavistock road, to the north of the town.

There is mention of the ancient landmark of Nun's Cross (or Siward's Cross) as early as 1280, in documents concerning ownership of Buckland Abbey lands. Over 7ft (2.1m) high, it stands on the route of the Abbot's Way – between Buckfast Abbey and Tavistock – and marks the eastern boundary of Buckland Abbey lands. The word 'Siward' engraved on its eastern face may refer to the Earl of Northumberland who owned much land in this part of the country in Saxon times, or may indicate some connection to a family named Siward who lived nearby. 'Bocland' on the other face may be a reference to Buckland Abbey. The word 'Nun's' comes from the Celtic *nans*, meaning combe or valley.

The Devonport Leat is an amazing feat of engineering, carried out between 1793 and 1801 to improve water supplies to Devonport, now part of Plymouth, which at that time was being developed as a naval base. Originally 26½ miles (43km) long, it carried 2 million gallons (4.5 million litres) of water a day. Lined with granite slabs and conveying crystal-clear, fast-flowing water, today it provides an extremely attractive, level walking route through some otherwise fairly inhospitable terrain. The final part of the walk, back to Princetown, follows the abandoned railway track that Tyrwhitt planned to link Princetown with Plymouth. The line, the first iron railway in the county, opened in 1823. More of a tramway than a railway, the horse-drawn wagons carried coal and lime up from Plymouth, and took stone back. In 1881 commercial considerations caused the line to be taken over by the Princetown Railway Company. It reopened as a steam railway in 1883, until its eventual closure in 1956.

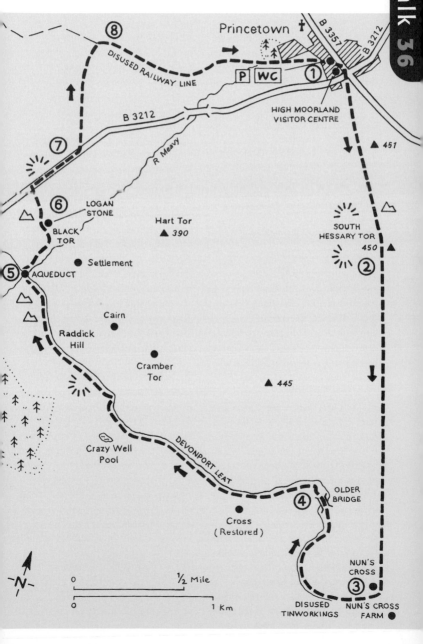

Walk 36 Directions

① Leave the car park past the toilets and turn right to pass the **High Moorland Visitor Centre**. Cross the road and follow the lane between the two pubs and their car parks behind. After 100yds (91m) a small gate leads to a broad gravelly track which ascends gently to **South Hessary Tor**, from which there are splendid views to **Plymouth Sound** ahead, and of the prison behind.

WHERE TO EAT AND DRINK ⓘ

The **Plume of Feathers** inn, originally a coaching house, is the oldest building in Princetown, dating from 1785. It has a campsite and camping barn and is a popular stopover for those exploring the moor on foot. Nearby is the **Railway Inn**. Both pubs are free houses, welcome families and serve good food.

---

② Follow the track as it drops down gently, passing boundary stones. It crosses two other tracks (look left for a view of the **Devonport Leat**) before dropping down to **Nun's Cross. Nun's Cross Farm** (originally a thatched house, c 1870) can be seen to the left.

③ Turn 90 degrees right at the cross to pick your way over a bumpy area of disused tin workings to find the end of the tunnel where the leat emerges. It's near the remains of a cottage under a beech and three hawthorn trees. Walk along the right bank of the leat.

④ Where the leat bends north cross it on **Older Bridge** (granite slabs) to walk along the left bank, with wonderful views of **Burrator reservoir** to the left. Follow the leat on; there are various crossing places and you should cross back to the right bank before descending to the valley of the **Meavy**; the leat picks up speed as it rushes downhill here, and the path is steep and rocky.

⑤ The Meavy is crossed via an aqueduct and the leat turns left. Take the grassy path right leading slightly uphill away from the river (there is a wealth of tin working evidence in the valley – worth an exploration). The path passes through a tumbledown granite wall; turn left and climb steeply up to **Black Tor**.

⑥ Go straight on past the **Logan Stone**, one of several on Dartmoor balanced in such a way that they can be rocked on their base, and on across open moorland to the road, with views of **Brentor, Swelltor Quarries** and the disused railway line ahead. Turn right at the road.

⑦ A few steps later, opposite the blocked off parking place, turn left and pick your way across tussocky grass, aiming for the mast on **North Hessary Tor**. This area is boggy in places, but passable.

⑧ At the railway track turn right and walk back to the edge of the town. The path splits, so keep left and through a small gate to join a tarmac road. Pass the **Devon Fire & Rescue Service** building to regain the car park on the right.

WHILE YOU'RE THERE ⓘ

Visit the **High Moorland Visitor Centre** (open 10AM–5PM), situated in the old Duchy Hotel, which you pass on Point ①. You'll find everything you ever wanted to know about the Dartmoor National Park here, and more besides. There's an information centre and shop, helpful staff, and a range of audio-visual and 'hands-on' displays.

The Mysteries of the Dewerstone

Industrial archaeology along the Plym – and a hard climb past the eerie Dewerstone Crags.

•DISTANCE•	3½ miles (5.7km)
•MINIMUM TIME•	1hr 45min
•ASCENT / GRADIENT•	180ft (55m) ▲▲ ▲▲ ▲▲
•LEVEL OF DIFFICULTY•	🚶🚶 🚶🚶 🚶
•PATHS•	Woodland paths, some rocky, and rough moorland, 4 stiles
•LANDSCAPE•	Oak woodland, deep river valley and open moorland
•SUGGESTED MAP•	aqua3 OS Outdoor Leisure 28 Dartmoor
•START / FINISH•	Grid reference: SX 555646
•DOG FRIENDLINESS•	Dogs can run free at all times, watch for sheep
•PARKING•	Free car park at Cadover Bridge
•PUBLIC TOILETS•	None on route

BACKGROUND TO THE WALK

This is a popular walk, not only because of its proximity to Plymouth, but also because of the wealth of obvious industrial archaeological interest. The best way to experience this is to start from Cadover Bridge, on the edge of the open moor towards the Lee Moor China Clay Works. You follow the route of the pipeline that carried the china clay in suspension from the works to the drying kilns at Shaugh Bridge (seen in the car park), via settling tanks, the remains of which are passed on the walk.

A Tale of Two Bridges

The area around Shaugh Bridge is a Site of Special Scientific Interest (SSSI), nationally important for plants and wildlife, and there is a constant conservation programme going on here. The bridge itself dates from the late 1820s, and replaces one that was badly damaged in January 1823. Cadover Bridge was named in a charter of 1291 as 'ponta de Cada worth', so its name probably derives from *cad*, Celtic for 'skirmish'. The Plym is also referred to as Plymma, from the Celtic *pilim*, 'to roll'.

This is definitely *not* the place to be on a black winter's night – the Devil (locally known as 'Dewer') has long been associated with the Dewerstone. The Devil's fearsome pack of wisht-hounds are said to roam the desolate moors at night, seeking unrepentant sinners, whom they drive over the edge of the crags to the Devil waiting below. One of the more unpleasant legends associated with this distinctive granite formation tells of how an old farmer met the Devil carrying a sack near the rock and, not recognising him, asked if he'd had a good day's hunting. The Devil is said to have laughed, and to have given the farmer the sack. The farmer, delighted, rushed home – only to find that the sack contained the body of his son. And beware, the woods near the Dewerstone are said to be haunted at night by a huge, evil dog with red eyes. Such stories are common in moorland areas, and perhaps date back to a time when wolves still inhabited the more remote parts of the country. Their eventual extinction in Britain was largely due to this process of demonisation.

Ancient Remains

There are Bronze Age hut circles and cairns on Wigford Down, dating to at least 1000 BC, and Iron Age fortifications protecting the summit of the ridge. Cadover Cross, passed on Point ⑧, is an ancient restored cross – the modern shaft is made of red granite – set on the line of the Monastic Way between Plympton and Tavistock. It was found lying recumbent in 1873 and re-erected, only to fall and be put up again in 1915, set in a large socket stone. It stands over 7ft 6in (2m) tall.

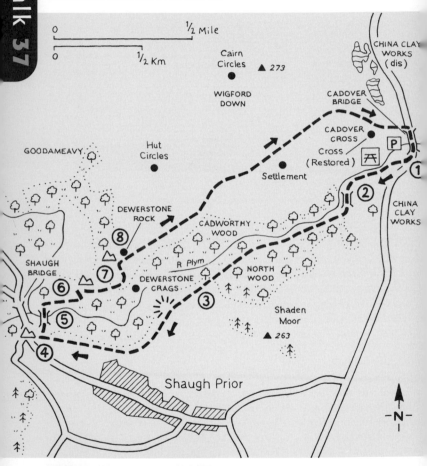

Walk 37 Directions

① From the car park, walk away from **Cadover Bridge**, with the river on your right. Cross over a stile into a willow plantation; the path here is rocky and muddy in places but the river beside you is always delightful, and you will come across lots of great picnic spots.

② A wooden ladder down a bank leads to a short stretch of pasture. A stile and footbridge leads into **North Wood** oak woodland. There is a choice of paths here; keep to the one with the large pipe set in the ground.

③ Leave **North Wood** over a stile and follow the path through an open brackeny area; the **Plym** is far

Walk 37

below on the right. Note the group of **Dewerstone Crags** ahead on the other side of the valley. The path leads into mixed silver birch and oak past a ruined building, then forks. Take the right fork slightly downhill to a small track and gate.

④ Turn right inside the wire fence, following the footpath sign 'Shaugh Bridge'. Stay within the woods as the path twists downhill and you can hear the river below right. The path leads over a stile past a notice 'Hazardous Area: Proceed with Caution' – this part can be slippery, but it's not that bad! You pass a settling tank (right), and the path ends at a road.

⑤ Turn immediately right and take the left fork then down steps into **Shaugh Bridge** car park. Turn right to walk through the car park towards the river.

⑥ Cross the river via the railed wooden footbridge to enter **Goodameavy** (National Trust). Follow the path right. It becomes a

> **WHERE TO EAT AND DRINK** ⓘ
> There's often an **ice cream van** in the car park at both Cadover Bridge and Shaugh Bridge. Formerly the old Church House, the **Royal Oak** at Meavy, a free house with good food and attractively sited tables outside, is over 500 years old and is set on the village green near the famous 1,000-year-old oak tree from which it takes its name. Meavy can be found on the way to Burrator Reservoir north of Cadover Bridge.

restored rocky track leading above the river and winds steeply uphill so take your time. Where the path goes straight ahead and there is also a sharp bend right, keep right and forever uphill until you see the top of the **Dewerstone Crags** through the trees right.

⑦ At this point the path becomes a rocky scramble left and up to leave the woods and onto open moorland to reach **Dewerstone Rock**, with glorious views.

⑧ Turn 90 degrees right at the rock and follow the broad central grassy path along the ridge to pass **Oxen Tor** and over **Wigford Down**, keeping **Cadworthy Wood** and the **Plym Valley** right. Keep straight on to the boundary wall of the wood, then left to follow the wall around fields. Eventually the wall veers right and you walk downhill past **Cadover Cross** with views of the china clay works beyond. Head towards the bridge, cross over on the road and walk back to your car.

> **WHILE YOU'RE THERE** ⓘ
> **Buckland Abbey**, in the Tavy Valley to the west of Yelverton, has strong associations with Sir Francis Drake. It was originally a small Cistercian monastery, and the house incorporates the remains of the 13th-century abbey church. There is a superb monastic barn, and delightful gardens and estate walks. Buckland Abbey is managed jointly by Plymouth City Council and the National Trust.

> **WHAT TO LOOK FOR** ⓘ
> The **Dewerstone Crags** provide the best middle-grade climbing in Dartmoor, and you are almost bound to see climbers from this walk. The main crag, **Devil's Rock**, rises 150ft (46m) from the banks of the Plym; to the right lie the isolated Needle and Upper and Lower Raven buttresses. Evocative names for the many routes here include *Hagar the Horrible*, *If I Should Fall...* and *Knucklecracker!* In 1960 a climber found a late Bronze Age (*c* 1000 BC) drinking vessel here.

Walk 38

Dartmoor's Highest Tors

A view of Yes Tor and High Willhays – without having to climb them – and an ancient oak woodland.

•DISTANCE•	4¼ miles (7km)
•MINIMUM TIME•	2hrs 45min
•ASCENT / GRADIENT•	722ft (220m) ▲▲▲
•LEVEL OF DIFFICULTY•	🚶🚶 🚶🚶 🚶🚶
•PATHS•	Grassy tracks and open moorland
•LANDSCAPE•	Reservoir, ancient oak woodland and open moorland
•SUGGESTED MAP•	aqua3 OS Outdoor Leisure 28 Dartmoor
•START / FINISH•	Grid reference: SX 563917
•DOG FRIENDLINESS•	Dogs can run free at all times, watch for sheep
•PARKING•	Car park at Meldon Reservoir (voluntary contributions)
•PUBLIC TOILETS•	At car park

BACKGROUND TO THE WALK

If you want to get a 'quick fix' and to experience examples of almost everything that Dartmoor has to offer, but fairly easily and in a relatively short time – then this is the walk for you. Within 10 minutes of the A30 as it races past Okehampton you can get the lot: a tranquil reservoir, a sparkling river and waterfall tumbling though a beautiful tree-lined valley, wide expanses of open moorland, an area of ancient lichen-encrusted oak woodland and a great view of the highest tors on the moor – and all without expending too much effort. You don't have to tramp for miles over unhospitable moorland or get to grips with a compass to get a real feel of the moor. **Note:** Be very careful if attempting this walk in mist.

Black Tor Copse
Owned by the Duchy of Cornwall, this is one of the best areas of ancient high altitude oak woodland in Britain, and was established as a National Nature Reserve in 1996. There is a huge variety of mosses and lichens covering the granite boulders from which the stunted oaks emerge – and the whole place is enchanting. It makes a wonderful focus for the walk. There are two other areas of upland woodland on the moor – at Piles Copse in the Erme Valley and at Wistman's Wood by the side of the West Dart River just north of Two Bridges. In all three places the oaks have remained ungrazed because the clutter of granite boulders beneath has protected them from the ravages of the local sheep. Black Tor Copse feels little visited and remote – the atmosphere is quite magical.

Dartmoor's Highest Tors
Dartmoor is basically a huge granite intrusion, pushed up through surrounding sedimentary rocks, formed in the same way as Bodmin Moor in Cornwall and the Isles of Scilly. Where it is exposed to the elements this raised granite plateau has been weathered into giant blocks, creating the tors so characteristic of the area. The highest part of the moor lies in the north east corner just south of the A30, where it rises to 2,037ft (621m) at High Willhays, seen from this walk. The average height of the moor, however, is around 1,200ft (366m).

Railway Stone

Sold by British Rail after privatisation, Meldon Quarry is around 200 years old, and was originally mined for a range of minerals. Tin, copper, limestone, roadstone and aplite, arsenic, copper, granite and churt have all come from here. The Black Down copper mine was in operation in the 19th century, as was the Hornfeld Quarry, which produced ballast for the new railways in the area. The quarry today produces ballast, roadstone, concrete aggregates and building stone, and covers 235 acres (95ha).

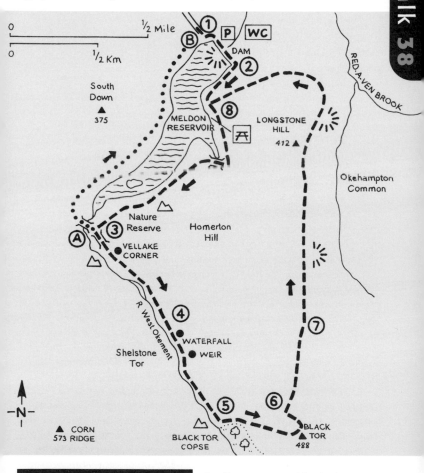

Walk 38 Directions

① Walk up the stone steps by the toilets, through the gate and left on a tarmac way towards the dam, signposted 'Bridleway to Moor'. Cross over the dam.

② Turn right along a stony track. You will soon see a stile (right)

leading to a waterside picnic area. Don't go over the stile, but leave the track here to go straight on, following the edge of the reservoir through a little side valley and over a small footbridge. The narrow path undulates to a steepish descent at the end of the reservoir to meet the broad marshy valley of the **West Okement River**; the swell of **Corn Ridge** 1,762ft (537m) lies ahead.

Walk 38

③ Cross the small wooden footbridge and take the narrow flinty path along the left edge of the valley, keeping to the bottom of the steep slope on your left. The path broadens uphill and becomes grassy as it rounds **Vellake Corner** above the tumbling river below right.

④ At the top of the hill the track levels and **Black Tor Copse** can be glimpsed ahead. Follow the river upstream past a waterfall and weir, right of a granite enclosure, and along the left bank through open moorland to enter **Black Tor Copse** – a wonderful picnic spot.

> **WHAT TO LOOK FOR** ⓘ
> There is clear evidence of the military presence on Dartmoor from this walk. As you admire the view over the Red-a-Ven Valley you will notice a line of red and white posts running along the hillside, which marks the boundary of the live firing ranges in this part of the moor. These are used for training on a limited number of days each year, and you can walk within the ranges outside these times – so long as you are sensible and take care not to touch any strange objects you might find.

⑤ Retrace your steps out of the trees and veer right around the copse edge, uphill aiming for the left outcrop of **Black Tor** on the

> **WHILE YOU'RE THERE** ⓘ
> Have a look at **Meldon Viaduct**, which you can see easily from the dam. This is a scheduled ancient monument dating from 1874, when the London & South Western Railway line was extended from Exeter to Lydford. Standing 150ft (45.7m) high and 541ft (165m) long, it was originally constructed in wrought iron, and now carries a National Cycle Route. The line from Meldon to Exeter is still used for quarry traffic.

ridge above. Pick your way through the bracken to gain the tor; there's no definite path here, but it's straightforward. The right outcrop rises 1,647ft (502m).

⑥ Return to the flattish grassy area north of the tor. Turn right to continue directly away from the river valley behind, aiming for a fairly obvious track visible ahead over **Longstone Hill**. To find the track go slightly downhill from the tor to meet a small stream. Turn left, then right towards three granite blocks marking the track.

⑦ The intermittent track runs straight across open moor, with good views of the quarry ahead. Where the **Red-a-Ven Brook Valley** appears below right, enjoy the view of (left to right) **Row Tor**, **West Mill Tor** and **Yes Tor**. **High Willhays**, Dartmoor's highest tor, lies just out of sight to the right. The track veers left around the end of the hill and drops back to the reservoir.

⑧ Turn right to rejoin the track back over the dam and back to the car park.

An Easier Return via Meldon Reservoir

A gentler way back, avoiding the climb to Black Tor.
See map and information panel for Walk 38

•DISTANCE•	3¼ miles (5.2km)
•MINIMUM TIME•	2hrs
•ASCENT / GRADIENT•	295ft (90m)
•LEVEL OF DIFFICULTY•	

Walk 39 Directions (Walk 38 option)

If, after your picnic, you feel that you can't handle the steep ascent to **Black Tor** and you'd rather just amble back to your car, there's a simple (and downhill) route home, which gives you another chance to enjoy breathtaking views over the reservoir. Retrace your steps from **Black Tor Copse** back down the right bank of the **West Okement River**, to pass the waterfall and return to **Vellake Corner**.

The valley of the West Okement River is extremely lovely here; the river rushes through a narrow, deep channel, over a tumble of granite boulders, under oak, hazel and willow trees. When you reach the footbridge at Point ③ turn left (Point Ⓐ) and cross the river on the stone bridge.

Climb over a stile, then right up steps, and follow the path to the right, to a gate marked 'Reservoir Walk Meldon Car Park'. The route from here on is very easy, and runs above the reservoir with some great views over the island at the southern end, and ahead towards the dam. The path ends at a gate.

Cross the path to a second gate, then left (Point Ⓑ) and immediately right into the car park. The reservoir was formed by the damming of the West Okement River, and the dam was built between 1970 and 1972, creating this beautiful landscape. The reservoir, covering an area of 4,100 acres (1,660ha), acts as a top-up supply during low river flows at nearby Prewley Treatment Works. The dam is most impressive – 660ft (201m) long and 145ft (44.25m) high, and cost £1.6m.

It's quite fun to go down the steps beneath the dam to have a look at the pretty **West Okement River** as it flows away down the valley – but remember that there are 191 steps back up to the top again.

WHERE TO EAT AND DRINK
There's often an **ice cream van** in the car park, and plenty of pubs in Okehampton. There's also the wonderful **Café Noir** in Red Lion Yard (just off Okehampton's main street) which serves excellent food and is something a little unusual for this part of Devon.

Walk 40

On the Tarka Trail without a Mountain Bike in Sight!

From the old market town of Hatherleigh to the idyllic village of Iddesleigh.

•DISTANCE•	7 miles (11.3km)
•MINIMUM TIME•	3hrs
•ASCENT / GRADIENT•	245ft (75m) ▲▲▲
•LEVEL OF DIFFICULTY•	🚶 🚶 🚶
•PATHS•	Fields and country lanes
•LANDSCAPE•	Rolling farmland and wooded valleys
•SUGGESTED MAP•	aqua3 OS Explorer 113 Okehampton
•START / FINISH•	Grid reference: SS 541044
•DOG FRIENDLINESS•	Dogs should be kept under control at all times, livestock in some fields
•PARKING•	Main car park in Hatherleigh
•PUBLIC TOILETS•	In the square, Market Street, Hatherleigh

Walk 40 Directions

The Tarka Trail, attributed to North Devon author Henry Williamson's classic book *Tarka the Otter*, runs for 180 miles (290km) through peaceful countryside, signed, most appropriately, with an otter paw. The trail covers a huge area, from Okehampton on the edge of Dartmoor, across the course of the Taw and Torridge rivers, to Ilfracombe on the coast, and east to Lynton and Exmoor. It forms a large figure-of-eight, following the old Barnstaple-to-Bideford railway line, various rights of way and permissive paths, and provides excellent opportunities for quiet exploration.

This route follows a part of the trail that is only open to walkers, and starts in the market town of **Hatherleigh**, an important centre for North and West Devon. Originally a Saxon settlement, the

town developed as a staging post on the main route from Bideford to Exeter, and to Plymouth. A great fire in 1840 destroyed much of the early fabric of the town.

Leave the car park (look out for the wonderful 'Sheep' sculpture) and turn left up **Bridge Street** and then **Market Street**, walking past the square and the parish church (St John the Baptist – now beautifully restored after the mid-15th century

WHAT TO LOOK FOR ⓘ
Although sightings are still rare, there's no doubt that **otter** numbers in Devon are on the increase – and any walk along the Tarka Trail instantly brings this charismatic creature to mind. The otter was widespread as recently as the 1950s but, following a sharp decline in numbers, conservation schemes have had to be introduced to sustain viable populations. One of Britain's few native carnivores, the otter is characterised by its powerful body (36in/90cm) and strong tail (16in/40cm), and much of its appeal lies in its apparent ability to have fun.

Walk 40

54ft (16.5m) spire plunged through the roof of the nave in the storms of January 1990).

At the top of the hill follow the road left, then turn right up **Sanctuary Lane** (signed 'to public footpath'). The lane climbs steeply; ignore all footpath signs until you pass **Wingate** at the hilltop; the lane bends sharp left. Go straight ahead through a gate into a field, signed 'Tarka Trail'. Walk straight across the field, through two gates, then across the next, keeping left of four big oak trees.

Leave the boggy field through a gate and pass through a coniferous plantation, over a footbridge and kissing gate and into a field. Walk straight over that field, over a stile and through the grounds of **Groves Fishleigh**. Go down the drive and through the gateposts to a T-junction. Turn right towards **Arnold's Fishleigh**. At the edge of the farm buildings turn sharp right (footpath sign) through a gate/stile into a small orchard. Turn left, then out over a stile and plank bridge under big oaks. Turn left and at the end of the field cross the stile, then keep right down the next field. Turn right through a gate/stile, then left through the next gateway, and follow the track downhill to cross the **Okement River** via a cantilevered gate/wooden bridge.

Turn left and walk along the riverbank, then right at the hedge. Go through the next gate, across the corner of the field and through a gate onto a green lane, running uphill. Follow footpath signs right through a gate, and cross the field to **Nethercott Barton**. Go through

the gate, turn left and follow the track uphill (note **Nethercott House** on the left). When the track meets a lane, turn left.

At **Parsonage Gate**, turn right down the drive to **Rectory Farm**, then right at the gates before the farmhouse. Pass through a metal gate to cross the farmyard, then through a gate (marked by an otter paw) and straight ahead. Take the right-hand gate at the end of that field (views left to **Iddesleigh**), and follow the muddy track downhill. Leave the field through a gate onto a green lane. Turn left at the tarmac lane and uphill. Turn right opposite the 15th-century **St James' Church**, then left to the pub.

> ### WHERE TO EAT AND DRINK ⓘ
> The **Tally Ho** on Market Street is both inn and brewery, and visitors can be shown around the brewery on request. Brews such as Tarka's Tipple, Midnight Madness and Nutters may well tempt you in. There's a good range of food, and a beer garden, but children under 14 and dogs are not allowed in the bar. The 15th-century **Duke of York** at Iddesleigh is a classic, unspoilt country pub, with a reputation for excellent food and a homely atmosphere.

Note: For a different route home, retrace your steps down the lane from the church, and keep going until **Vellaford Cross**. Turn right along the lane on **Hatherleigh Moor** – the views south to Dartmoor should not be missed. Pass the 1860 **Hatherleigh Monument**, commemorating the distinguished actions of Lt Col William Morris at the Charge of the Light Brigade. Past the Hatherleigh sign, turn right down **Park Road** to reach the top of **Market Street**.

The Devil versus the Church

A climb up to the Church of St Michael de Rupe at Brent Tor in West Devon.

•DISTANCE•	4 miles (6.4km)
•MINIMUM TIME•	2hrs
•ASCENT / GRADIENT•	425ft (130m) ▲▲▲
•LEVEL OF DIFFICULTY•	🚶🚶 🚶 🚶
•PATHS•	Tracks and green lanes, open fields and lanes
•LANDSCAPE•	Open moorland and rolling farmland
•SUGGESTED MAP•	aqua3 OS Explorer 112 Launceston & Holsworthy
•START / FINISH•	Grid reference: SX 495800
•DOG FRIENDLINESS•	On the lead on road at Brent Tor, some livestock in fields
•PARKING•	Lay-by past cattle grid outside Mary Tavy on moorland road to North Brentor village
•PUBLIC TOILETS•	At car park, Brent Tor

BACKGROUND TO THE WALK

Anyone exploring western Dartmoor cannot fail to notice a conical peak, topped with a tower, protruding high above the rolling fields and woodlands towards the Cornish border. This strange natural formation is Brent Tor and, surprisingly, has nothing to do with the granite tors of Dartmoor. It is a remnant of the mass of lava that poured out onto the seabed here over 300 million years ago, when the area was a shallow sea. The softer rocks around have been eroded away over the millennia, leaving behind this extraordinary landmark 1,100ft (334m) above sea level. The name is thought to derive either from the Anglo-Saxon *brene*, meaning 'beacon' (to burn) or from the Celtic *bryn* (hill or mound). Lying just inside the National Park boundary, it provides the perfect focus for a relaxing exploration of this quiet corner of West Devon.

A Spectacular Location
The 13th-century Church of St Michael de Rupe ('of the rock') was originally built by Robert Giffard, Lord of the Manor of Lamerton and Whitchurch, around 1130. Rebuilt towards the end of the 13th century, the 40ft (12.25m) tower was added during the 15th century, and it is the fourth smallest complete parish church in England. Services are held on Sunday evenings from Easter to September, and the views from here are quite breathtaking. A similarly located church, St Michael's on the Mount at Glastonbury, is said to be linked to Brent Tor by a ley line.

Angry Devil
It is said that while the church was being built the Devil himself hurled stones from the top of the hill onto the unfortunate parishioners below. Another legend tells of how a wealthy 14th-century merchant vowed to build a church here in gratitude to St Michael for saving one of his cargoes from a terrible storm at sea. The Devil came every night to destroy the building work, so the merchant called in St Michael to help again. The saint hid behind Cox Tor, to the south east, and hurled a boulder at the Devil, so chasing him away. In return the church was dedicated to St Michael.

North Brentor was added to the parish in 1880, and all burials then took place at Christ Church in the village, since the soil on top of Brent Tor was too thin to accommodate a decent grave. Burial logistics seem to have featured strongly in this part of Devon over the years. The Church of St Petroc at Lydford, originally a Saxon foundation, used to hold the only consecrated ground close to the northern part of the moor. Bodies were carried across the moor for burial along a route known as the Lich Way (*lich* meaning corpse), from which comes lychgate, the entrance gate to many churchyards.

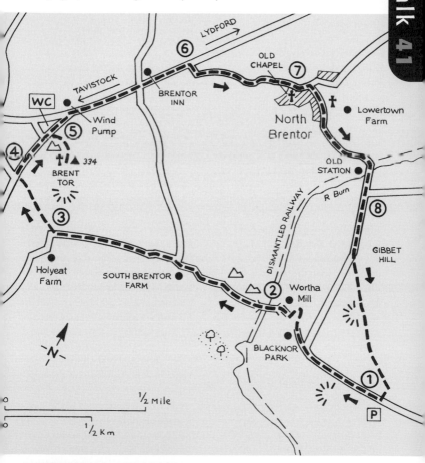

Walk 41 Directions

① Walk straight ahead from your car towards **Brent Tor**, which positively invites you to visit it. Where the lane veers right turn left along an unfenced lane (dead end and weak bridge signs). Go gently downhill and over a cattle grid. The tarmac lane becomes a gravelly track and passes **Blacknor Park** (left), to cross the old railway line.

② The stony track runs steeply uphill, levels off and runs into a green lane. At the next T-junction of tracks turn left to pass **South Brentor Farm** and a lane (right), and keep straight on slightly uphill – under beech trees – to pass '**Hillside**' on the left.

Walk 41

③ Just past a pretty white cottage on the left the lane bends sharp left. Turn right through a wooden gate (no sign) and along the bottom of the field, keeping the hedge left. **Brent Tor** is above to the right. Pass through double metal gates to meet the **Tavistock to Lydford road** – take care.

④ Turn right to reach the car park, toilets and information board for **Brent Tor** on the left.

⑤ Turn right and take the steep path up to the church – it's always windy up here – then retrace your steps to the road and turn right to pass the **Brentor Inn** on your left.

⑥ When you reach two white cottages on either side of the road, turn right down a tarmac lane signposted 'Brentor and Mary Tavy'. The lane runs gently downhill, with the moor rising steeply up behind the village ahead. This western edge of the moor is very different from the eastern side, where there is usually a long drive-in along wooded river valleys.

WHILE YOU'RE THERE ⓘ
Visit **Lydford**, signposted off the A386 to the north. It was a Saxon fortress town, with its own mint in the 9th century. Lydford Castle, actually the moor's infamous stannery prison, is worth a visit. Just down the road is the National Trust's Lydford Gorge, where the crashing waterfalls and whirlpools of the River Lyd – the most impressive being the Devil's Cauldron – can be seen from a number of woodland walks. The 98ft (30m) White Lady waterfall is spectacular.

WHAT TO LOOK FOR ⓘ
Just south west of Brent Tor is an enclosed area of mounds and depressions, all that remains of a 19th-century **manganese mine**, a major source of employment from 1815–56. The manganese was used in the production of glass, bleach and steel, and was shipped out down the River Tamar from Morwellham Quay.

⑦ At the edge of the houses go straight on, keeping the old chapel right, until you reach the 1914-18 **war memorial**. Turn right slightly downhill to pass the phone box, church and village hall. Follow the lane as it veers right to cross the old railway line. You can see the old station complete with platform canopy below you to the right.

⑧ Pass over the cattle grid onto the open moor, and up the lane. Where the lane bends right and you see two big granite gateposts in the beech-lined wall right, cut left diagonally over the edge of **Gibbet Hill** on an indistinct grassy track. The lane leads back to the car, but this is a more pleasant route. At the crest of the hill you will see your route back to your car on the lane below to the right.

WHERE TO EAT AND DRINK ⓘ
The **Brentor Inn** can be found after Point ⑤, before the turning to North Brentor. It's a free house, with a family room and beer garden. If you drive north to Lydford go to the 16th-century **Castle Inn** (hotel and restaurant), which is a superb place for lunch, dinner, or to stay the night. There is also a **National Trust restaurant** at Lydford Gorge.

North Devon Coast Classic

A walk of contrasts: Lee Bay – the 'fuchsia valley' – and craggy Morte Point.

•DISTANCE•	8 miles (12.9km)
•MINIMUM TIME•	4hrs 15min
•ASCENT / GRADIENT•	426ft (130m) ▲▲▲
•LEVEL OF DIFFICULTY•	👫 👫 👫
•PATHS•	Fields, tracks and coast path, 15 stiles
•LANDSCAPE•	Coastal farmland, wooded valleys and cliff tops
•SUGGESTED MAP•	aqua3 OS Explorer 139 Bideford, Ilfracombe & Barnstaple
•START / FINISH•	Grid reference: SS 452458
•DOG FRIENDLINESS•	Dogs should be kept under control at all times
•PARKING•	Car park at Mortehoe
•PUBLIC TOILETS•	Lee Bay and behind church at Mortehoe

BACKGROUND TO THE WALK

This walk is included because it is simply beautiful – there's no other word for it. Although this part of the North Devon coast is extremely popular with holidaymakers, you can escape pretty quickly. Just a few minutes' walk from the car park you will see tremendous views of the coast opening up to the left. On a clear day you can see the Gower Peninsula in South Wales, and within half an hour you've left civilisation behind. It's a wonderfully varied route, too. You'll pass the ancient farmstead at Damage Barton to cross a lovely area of unimproved meadowland and penetrate deep down into the wooded Borough valley to discover the secluded cove at Lee Bay. This is followed by a tough walk along the coast path to the jagged headland of Morte Point, off which the white horses of the strong tidal race rage. The dreaded Morte Stone lies out here, causing the demise of no less than five ships over the winter of 1852. It's a walk that shouldn't be rushed, and it won't be crowded – take it gently and revel in the peace and solitude.

Fuchsia Valley

Lee Bay is a very special place. The small village, with many cottages dating from the 16th and 17th centuries, lies along a narrow, winding lane running down to an attractive rocky cove. It's one of those places that many people never discover. Its sheltered position has encouraged a wealth of flowers, including hedges of naturalised fuchsia bushes.

Tennyson said of St Mary Magdalene Church in Mortehoe 'that tower of strength which stood four-square to all the winds that blew', and you certainly get a feeling of solidity when you look at the little Norman church, with its tower dating from around 1270. In a sheltered position just inland from Morte Point, and with an isolated feel despite its proximity to the village, it was probably founded in 1170 by Sir William de Tracey, and it may be his tomb that lies in the south transcept. The church is dark, pretty and simple. There is some glorious stained glass, and a superb mosaic chancel arch, completed in 1905.

If the tide's out when you reach Lee Bay, there's an exciting alternative to the route given at Point ⑤. When you reach the cove, walk across the beach left, near the cliff, and along a deep gully through the rocks – with wonderful rockpools – to reach Sandy Cove. You rejoin the main route by climbing up a steep flight of wooden steps to the coast path.

Walk 42

MORTE POINT

WINDY COVE

⑧

½ Mile

½ Km

N

ROCKHAM BAY

GRUNTA BEACH

WC ▲ 137

Mortehoe

P

①

ROCKHAM BAY HOTEL

②

▲ 129

EASEWELL FARM CAMPSITE

YARDE FARM

Twitchen House

③

DAMAGE BARTON FARM

BULL POINT LIGHTHOUSE

⑦

Bull Point

Standing Stone

Standing Stone

Standing Stone

WARCOMBE FARM

④

Quarry Cottage

OPEN ACCESS AREA

Doctor's Cleave

Manor House

⑤

BOROUGH VALLEY

Lee

⑥

THE GRAMPUS PUB

BOROUGH WOOD

Windcutter Hill

LEE BAY

Walk 42 **Directions**

① Take the lane opposite signposted 'Lighthouse & Lee'. Pass **Rockham Bay Hotel** to reach the lane end at the private road to **Bull Point lighthouse**.

② Follow footpath signs through the gate (right) across **Easewell Farm** campsite and through the campsite complex – it feels odd but it's allowed. Leave the buildings through a gate (with a pond right) and cross the field to **Yarde Farm** via a stile. Turn left immediately along a rocky track slightly uphill to a gate/stile into a field. Keep the wall on the left, and cross a stile in the muddy bottom corner (keep right to avoid deepest mud) onto a farm track.

③ Turn left, following signs through **Damage Barton Farm** veering right towards **Warcombe Farm** and **Borough Wood**. After a few steps a footpath sign on the building ahead directs you left. Soon after, another sign points right, then left through a gate. Walk uphill through a scrubby area to reach a footpath post. Go right towards another signpost, fork right through a rough area, then follow the wooden posts through a gate. Cross the field to the hedge and look for the next signpost atop a small hill. Cross over the stile in the next hedge, then walk across the field to a lane via a stile.

④ Cross the lane and over a stile, leading into an 'Open Access area' and viewpoint. Follow signs to **Lee** across the meadow. Cross over a stile and go steeply downhill into the wooded **Borough Valley**. At the bottom turn left.

⑤ Follow the valley down to emerge from the woods and turn right over a bridge and stile. Cross the field then a stile and turn right up the lane to **The Grampus** pub.

⑥ Retrace your steps down the lane past toilets to the rocky cove at **Lee Bay**. Turn left steeply uphill and join the coast path through a gate. Follow footpath signs to reach a stile/footbridge/stile at the bottom of a deep combe, then up steps and over a stile into another combe and rocky cove. Cross the footbridge and walk up to reach **Bull Point**.

⑦ Follow the footpath signs left of the lighthouse towards **Morte Point**. Go through a gate down into a combe – there are 97 steps up the other side. Cross **Windy Lag** and down to **Rockham Bay**, where steps lead to the beach. Cross two stiles and walk on to reach **Morte Point**.

⑧ Follow the coast path signs past **Windy Cove**. Cross over a stile, walk past **Grunta Beach**, then follow signs left, steeply uphill, to join the road just below **Mortehoe**. Proceed uphill and veer right to the car park.

Walk 42

Walk 43

The Spectacular Heddon Valley on Exmoor

Hanging oakwoods, rushing rivers, and some of the highest cliffs in England.

•DISTANCE•	5 miles (8km)
•MINIMUM TIME•	2hrs 45min
•ASCENT / GRADIENT•	787ft (240m) ▲▲▲
•LEVEL OF DIFFICULTY•	🚶 🚶 🚶
•PATHS•	Wooded tracks, exposed coast path and quiet lanes, 2 stiles
•LANDSCAPE•	Deep, wooded river valleys and very high cliffs
•SUGGESTED MAP•	aqua3 OS Outdoor Leisure 9 Exmoor
•START / FINISH•	Grid reference: SS 655481
•DOG FRIENDLINESS•	Dogs to be kept under control at all times
•PARKING•	National Trust car park at Heddon Gate
•PUBLIC TOILETS•	Opposite car park

BACKGROUND TO THE WALK

Situated within the Exmoor National Park, yet still in Devon, the deeply wooded Heddon Valley, leading to the stark cleft in the coastline at Heddon's Mouth, is one of the most spectacular sights in the county. There is no obvious main route into the valley, which you reach by turning off the A39 between Blackmoor Gate and Lynton, and then winding your way down miles of narrow lanes.

Parracombe Church

The best and most evocative way in is to go through the pretty village of Parracombe. Stop for a while to have a look at Parracombe old church, where nothing has been changed from the late 18th century when a new church was built nearer the village, then follow the course of the Heddon river as it descends through beautiful oak woodland to reach Heddon Gate. Although only one third of the Exmoor National Park is in Devon, more than half of the National Park coastline lies within the county, and the stretch seen on this walk is the most awe-inspiring section. This walk is not recommended for anyone who suffers from vertigo, and dogs should be kept under tight control on the coast path stretch.

The National Trust and the West Exmoor Coast

The National Trust owns 2,000 acres (810ha) of land here, much of which is a Site of Special Scientific Interest. The extensive oak woodlands, deep combes, coastal heath and some of the highest cliffs in England combine to produce one of the most magnificent landscape areas in Devon. The land immediately to the west and east of Heddon's Mouth Cleave rises very steeply up scree-covered slopes to a staggering 820ft (250m), and Great Hangman, the highest cliff in southern England at over 1,000ft (305m) lies just beyond Holdstone Down to the west. Exmoor, unlike Dartmoor, runs right up to the coast, and the cliff scenery towards Combe Martin on this walk is superb. There's no access to the sea between Heddon's Mouth and Combe Martin, 5 miles (8km) to the west. The National Trust information centre at Heddon Gate is excellent, and includes a very effective relief model of the area.

There is a huge amount of wildlife interest here. The West Exmoor coastline holds one of only two colonies of razorbill, guillemot and kittiwake in North Devon. In the oak woodland you can expect to see green and lesser spotted woodpeckers, pied flycatchers, wood warblers and nuthatches, among others. The Heddon Valley is managed by English Nature to encourage the right plants for butterflies, in particular the rare high brown fritillary, and dark green and silver washed fritillaries.

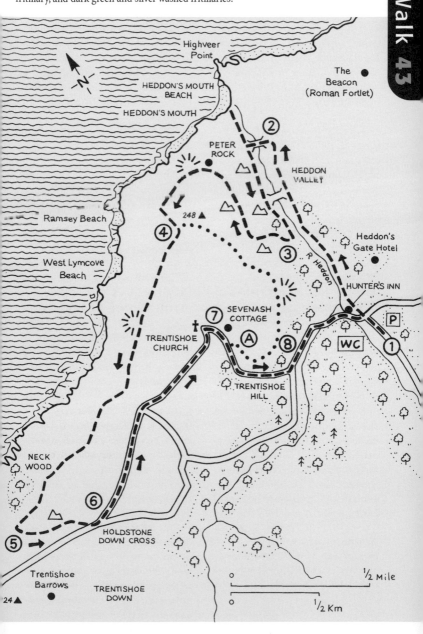

Walk 43 Directions

Walk 43

① Walk towards **Hunter's Inn**. To the right of the building you will see a wooded track, signed 'Heddon's Mouth' through a gate. Walk down the track, which soon splits; keep left, signed '**Heddon's Mouth beach**'. Keep to the gritty path nearest the river. The coast path (unsigned) joins this path from the right.

② Turn left over a wooden footbridge, then turn right and walk towards the coast to reach the 19th-century lime kiln above the rocky beach. Retrace your steps, keeping the river on your left, to pass two footbridges. Keep going until a coast path sign to **Combe Martin** directs you right, sharply uphill.

③ A steep zig-zag climb is rewarded with amazing views across the valley and inland. Keep going along the narrow path, which runs parallel to the valley to reach the coast above **Heddon's Mouth**, then turns left to run towards **Peter Rock**. The cliffs here are over 650ft (200m) high and sheer, and the path is narrow and exposed – take care. Continue along the path, which runs inland to meet a wall.

④ Turn right, signed to **Combe Martin**. Follow coast path signs through a gate, then right, along a short wire-fenced section and then

over a stile to rejoin the cliff edge. Cross over a stile above **Neck Wood**, then leave National Trust lands via a stile and kissing gate. The coast path continues straight ahead.

⑤ Turn left and walk uphill, then left again where the path meets a wide grassy path. Proceed uphill, following the fence, to reach the rough parking area and lane at **Holdstone Down Cross**, on the edge of **Trentishoe Down**.

WHAT TO LOOK FOR

On the path from Point ④ you'll find an information board about the **Exmoor pony**. Of all the native breeds, this is the nearest to a truly wild equine. There are very few pure-breds left and attempts are being made to increase their numbers. They're used on Little Hangman, near Combe Martin, to encourage the regeneration of the heather moorland.

---

⑥ Turn left along the narrow lane, following signs for **Trentishoe church** (the signpost here misleadingly points back the way you have come). Walk along the lane until you see the church above you on the left – this is a good place for a break.

⑦ Continue downhill below **Sevenash Cottage** to pass the point where there is an '**Access to coast path**' sign pointing left. Walk straight on down **Trentishoe Hill** (this lane is unsuitable for vehicles) which runs through wooded **Trentishoe Cleave**.

WHERE TO EAT AND DRINK

The **Fox and Goose Inn** at Parracombe is an interesting building, with good food. The **Hunter's Inn**, built in 1904 on the site of the original thatched inn, which was destroyed by fire in 1895, is a free house, with accommodation. **Ice creams** are available at the National Trust shop.

---

⑧ Turn left at the valley bottom by two pretty white cottages. Walk along the lane past a footpath sign to the **Heddon Valley** on the left, cross over a small river, and then over the **Heddon river** just before the **Hunter's Inn**. Turn right to find your car.

The Tiny Church at Trentishoe

An easier way to reach St Peter's Church, high above the Heddon Valley.
See map and information panel for Walk 43

•DISTANCE•	3¼ miles (5.2km)
•MINIMUM TIME•	2hrs
•ASCENT / GRADIENT•	787ft (240m) ▲▲▲
•LEVEL OF DIFFICULTY•	🚶 🚶 🚶

Walk 44 Directions (Walk 43 option)

If the rigours of the coast path get too much for you, you can escape from the cliffs soon after **Peter Rock**, and take this shorter way to the simple church at Trentishoe.

At Point ④ on the main walk, turn left, signed to '**Trentishoe Church**'. This lovely, grassy, level path runs inland 720ft (220m) above the valley of the **River Heddon**, and the views over the deep combes that join the main valley are glorious. It's a very easy walk, and a welcome relief after the coast path.

The path meets the lane at Point Ⓐ (Point ⑦ – '**access to coast path' sign**). Turn right up the lane and, after 200yds (183m), you will see the church above the lane on the right. It's hard to work out why there should be a church here – it's in the middle of nowhere – but 96 people are recorded as living here in 1891. The church is mentioned in the Episcopal Register of 1260. The tiny castellated tower dates from the 15th century, as do parts of the west wall and north and south walls of the nave. Until alterations were

made at the end of the 19th century this was the smallest church in Devon. There's a wonderful musician's gallery, built in 1771, and a lovely piece of information about the first organ, which was introduced in 1861 on condition that 'worthy parishioners are not asked to subscribe as they would expect to be allowed to join in the singing'! The hamlet also featured in RD Blackmore's novel *Clara Vaughan* which was published in 1864 and set in Trentishoe.

To rejoin the main route follow Points ⑦ and ⑧ from the church to your car.

WHILE YOU'RE THERE ⓘ

Have a look at another extraordinary piece of coastal landscape, at the **Valley of Rocks** just west of Lynton. This craggy dry valley is different from anywhere else on Exmoor, and is characterised by jagged sandstone tors, formed as a result of weathering processes over thousands of years. There is a pleasant walk into Lynton on the North Walk along the cliff edge from here. Look out for the feral goats that live amongst the rocky slopes. Although there were goats here in the 17th century, it seems that they were removed before being reintroduced in the late 19th century. They are now something of a tourist attraction.

Walk 45

Watersmeet and the Lynmouth Floods

The misleadingly tranquil waters of the Hoar Oak Water and East Lyn River once swelled up to biblical proportions in a catastrophic flood.

•DISTANCE•	3 miles (4.8km)
•MINIMUM TIME•	1hr 30min
•ASCENT / GRADIENT•	164ft (50m) ▲▲ ▲▲ ▲▲
•LEVEL OF DIFFICULTY•	🚶🚶 🚶🚶 🚶🚶
•PATHS•	Riverside paths, some stony
•LANDSCAPE•	Deep, narrow, wooded river valleys
•SUGGESTED MAP•	aqua3 OS Outdoor Leisure 9 Exmoor
•START / FINISH•	Grid reference: SS 740477
•DOG FRIENDLINESS•	Dogs should be kept under control at all times
•PARKING•	National Trust car park in grounds of Combe Park (hotel), Hillsford Bridge
•PUBLIC TOILETS•	At Watersmeet

Walk 45 Directions

Watersmeet, where the Hoar Oak Water and East Lyn river converge, is a very popular spot for visitors to this part of the Exmoor National Park, and the Watersmeet car park, within spitting distance of the beauty spot on the A39, is always busy. There is a much more satisfying – and quieter – way of getting there, via an easy and scenic walk that skirts round the busiest paths. The National Trust owns

200 acres (800ha) of glorious countryside around Watersmeet – rocky cliffs, steep oak-wooded valleys, open moorland and rushing rivers. Much of the area has been designated as a Site of Special Scientific Interest and there are 38 miles (61km) of footpaths.

Leave the car park and turn left, then right to cross **Hillsford Bridge**. Turn immediately left through a gate to follow the right bank of the **Hoar Oak Water**, slightly downhill (signed '**Watersmeet**'). The valley sides here are extremely steep, and wooded – the river tumbles along a rocky ravine below. You pass a waterfall and viewing point left, and soon reach steps (left) leading to **Watersmeet**.

Continue along the path, veering right, to proceed up the right bank of the **East Lyn River**, past another path to **Watersmeet** and then a

> **ⓘ WHERE TO EAT AND DRINK**
> The National Trust café and restaurant in **Watersmeet House**, open April to October, offers a delicious selection of food and drink, and the garden provides a wonderful setting for tea. There is a large range of cafés, pubs and fish and chip establishments just down the road at Lynmouth and Lynton, but both can become extremely crowded during the holiday season.

lime kiln, used to burn limestone brought here by boat from South Wales. Ahead and above you can see the huge swell of **Countisbury Common**, rising to 1,125ft (343m).

In the early 18th century Daniel Defoe described Exmoor as 'a filthie barren waste', in keeping with contemporary views of wilderness areas. Few would agree with that notion today, but the landscape is certainly surprisingly dramatic for southern England – the East Lyn has cut deeply into the moorland plateau, and runs 600ft (200m) below. The path winds through beautiful semi-natural hanging oak woodland to reach a junction. Take the '**footpath to Rockford**' ahead, descending through a beech glade to regain the riverbank.

When **Ash Bridge** is reached, cross over and turn left, signed '**Fisherman's Path**'. You could go straight along the right bank to reach **Rockford**, and the **Rockford Inn**, within a mile (1.6km), cross there and return on the opposite bank but on the main route pass **Crook Pool** on a bend, then walk along the narrow, undulating path above the river.

Go past **Watersmeet House** and veer right around the garden fence. Notice the enormous Monterey pine here, in its last years, and its younger replacement. The popularity of the Romantic Movement in the late 18th century meant that landscapes such as Watersmeet and Lynmouth became attractive and fashionable. Revd WS Halliday bought the site in 1829, and built Watersmeet House as a secluded retreat and hunting lodge. Today it provides the perfect setting for a picturesque break.

Walk a little way down the right bank of the river to cross stone **Chiselcombe Bridge**, which was built from public subscriptions after the ancient bridge was destroyed in the famous flood. On 15 August 1952, a 40ft (12m) wall of water surged down into Lynmouth. Houses and bridges were swept away by the torrents of water, boulders and debris, and 34 people died. This followed a prolonged spell of exceptionally heavy rainfall, culminating in 9in (228mm) of rain falling on the moor in a 24-hour period – one of the three heaviest periods of rainfall ever recorded in the British Isles. Over 3 billion gallons (13.6 billion litres) of water fell into the area drained by the two rivers.

Once over the bridge turn left, and walk back up the riverbank. Cross back over the **Hoar Oak Water** on a wooden footbridge just above **Watersmeet**. Take the steps right, following signs '**Hillsford Bridge**', then right and retrace your steps upriver to the bridge and back to **Combe Park**.

WHAT TO LOOK FOR ⓘ

Both red and roe deer can be spotted in the woodlands around Watersmeet and the moors which rise above the river valleys. The **red deer** is Britain's largest native land animal, and a fully grown stag can stand as much as 48in (120cm) at the shoulder, with antlers up to 28in (70cm) long. Although their main stronghold lies in the Highlands of Scotland, they are found wild elsewhere in the country, including here in Devon. The smaller **roe deer** are extremely shy, and most likely to be seen at dawn or dusk. The bucks have small antlers, with short branches, and the species is characterised by a white patch on the rump, easily visible when the deer is startled and runs off.

Clovelly Without the Crowds

Pheasants and follies – and a different way into Clovelly.

•DISTANCE•	5 miles (8km)
•MINIMUM TIME•	2hrs 15min
•ASCENT / GRADIENT•	410ft (125m) ▲▲ ▲▲
•LEVEL OF DIFFICULTY•	👫 👫 👫
•PATHS•	Grassy coast path, woodland and farm tracks, 4 stiles
•LANDSCAPE•	Farmland, wooded coast path and deep combes
•SUGGESTED MAP•	aqua3 OS Explorer 126 Clovelly & Hartland
•START / FINISH•	Grid reference: SS 285259
•DOG FRIENDLINESS•	Dogs should be kept under control at all times
•PARKING•	National Trust car park at Brownsham
•PUBLIC TOILETS•	Clovelly Visitor Centre

BACKGROUND TO THE WALK

Everyone's heard about Clovelly. It's an extraordinary place – almost a folly itself – best seen very early in the morning, or at the end of the day when most of the visitors have gone home. Clinging precariously to the wooded cliffs on the long, virtually uninhabited stretch of inhospitable coastline between Bideford and Hartland Point, it has a timeless feel if you see it 'out of office hours', or in mid-winter. Once famous as the village where donkeys were used to carry goods – and people – from the quay up the perilously steep cobbled village street (the bed of an old watercourse), today it is best known as a tourist trap. Most people drive to the village and are drawn into the Visitor Centre car park at the top – but it's much more satisfying, and more fitting to Clovelly's situation, to walk in along the coast path from the National Trust lands at Brownsham to the west. The two 17th-century farmhouses of Lower and Higher Brownsham, now converted into holiday accommodation, lie just inland from one of the most unspoilt sections of the north Devon coastline. Although the walk is rarely out of the trees, you can still hear the pull and drag of the waves on the shingly beach far below.

Literary Connections

Charles Kingsley, social reformer and author of *Westward Ho!* and *The Water Babies*, lived in Clovelly as a child when his father was rector of All Saints Church. Clovelly featured heavily in *Westward Ho!*, published in 1855, and the world suddenly became aware of this remote village's existence. Up till then it had been reliant on herring fishing for its main source of income. Charles Dickens also mentioned Clovelly in *A Message from the Sea* (1860), so extending its new-found popularity.

Clovelly Court dates from around 1740, when the Hamlyns bought the Manor from the Carys, but was remodelled in Gothic style in 1790–5. The gardens are open daily from 10AM to 4PM, and there's an honesty box for an admission fee. The much restored 15th-century All Saints Church has a Norman porch, dating from around 1300, and many monuments to the Cary and Hamlyn families. Sir James Hamlyn, who died in 1829, was responsible for the building of the Hobby Drive, which runs for 3 miles (4.8km) along the cliffs east of Clovelly, and from which you get fantastic views of the harbour, 600ft (183m) below.

Walk 46 Directions

① Leave the car park over a stile opposite the entrance. Walk along the field and through a gate into woods. Follow signs 'Footpath to coast path' to pass a bench. Go straight on 'Mouth Mill & coast path'. Cross over a stile and on to meet the coast path.

② Go right over a stile into the field on Brownsham Cliff. There are good views ahead to **Morte Point**. Keep to the left edge, across a stile, down steps and left round the next field. Cross a stile and zig-zag downhill through woodland. When you leave the trees turn left towards the sea at **Mouth Mill**.

③ Follow the coast path across the stream by stepping stones. Clamber up the rocky gully left and turn right onto the gritty track, on a bend. Keep going left, uphill.

> **WHAT TO LOOK FOR** ⓘ
>
> Pheasants – and you don't have to look for them on this walk! You'll pass through much privately owned forestry, most of which is used for rearing pheasants. Britain's commonest game bird was introduced from Asia in the Middle Ages. The male is beautiful, with an iridescent green head and rich brown body. The female is smaller, duller and pale brown.

④ After 200yds (183m) follow coast path signs left, then immediately right. Go left up wooden steps to follow a narrow, wooded path uphill towards the cliffs below **Gallantry Bower**, with a 400ft (122m) drop into the sea.

⑤ Follow the signed path through woodland to pass the folly 'the Angel's Wings'. Where a path leads straight on to the church, keep left following signs and via a gate through the edge of **Clovelly Court** estate (right). Pass into laurel woods via a kissing gate. The path winds down and up past a brick-built

> **WHERE TO EAT AND DRINK** ⓘ
>
> There are several pubs in Clovelly, including the **Red Lion Hotel** down at the quay. At nearby Woolfardisworthy (Woolsery to the locals), there is the **Farmer's Arms**, serving good food, the **Manor Inn** – or fish and chips.

shelter, then through a kissing gate into a field. Keep to the left; through a gate and oak trees to meet the road at a big gate. Follow coast path signs on to the road that leads to the top of **Clovelly** village below the **Visitor Centre**.

⑥ Walk up deep, steep, ancient **Wrinkleberry Lane** (right of **Hobby Drive** ahead) to a lane, past the school and on to meet the road. Turn right; where the road bends right go through the gates to **Clovelly Court**. At the T-junction follow bridleway signs left ('**Court Farm & sawmills**') through the farm, through a metal gate (sometimes open) and along the track. Pass through a small wooded section and walk on to the hedge at the end of the field.

⑦ Turn right, then left though a gate (by a footpath sign). At the bottom of the field go through a gate into a plantation, downhill.

⑧ Turn left at the forest track, following bridleway signs. Turn right up the long, gradually ascending track to **Lower Brownsham Farm**. Turn left for the car park.

> **WHILE YOU'RE THERE** ⓘ
>
> Have a look at the charming cove at **Buck's Mills**, signposted off the A39 at Buck's Cross. There's free parking in the wooded valley just above the village. When herring and mackerel fishing declined in the 19th century local men travelled daily to Lundy to work in the quarry. The popularity of the surname Braund in the village is thought to result from seven Spanish sailors, wrecked at sea and washed up here at the time of the Spanish Armada. The Old Mill café displays interesting bits and pieces about the village.

A Tough Trek into Cornwall

A strenuous coastal walk to the Bush Inn at Morwenstow.

•DISTANCE•	5¾ miles (9.2km)
•MINIMUM TIME•	3hrs 30min
•ASCENT / GRADIENT•	328ft (100m) ▲▲▲
•LEVEL OF DIFFICULTY•	🚶 🚶 🚶
•PATHS•	Rugged coastal footpath, fields and tracks, 14 stiles
•LANDSCAPE•	Steeply undulating combes and cliff tops
•SUGGESTED MAP•	aqua3 OS Explorer 126 Clovelly & Hartland
•START / FINISH•	Grid reference: SS 213179
•DOG FRIENDLINESS•	Dogs to be kept under control at all times
•PARKING•	Welcombe Mouth, bumpy track passable with care
•PUBLIC TOILETS•	None on route

BACKGROUND TO THE WALK

This walk takes us over the border into Cornwall, along a rugged coastal route – and feels completely Cornish. The colours here are green and grey, and any sense of cosy, comfortable Devon is left far behind as you trudge steadily up and down the switchback coast path south from the stark, remote, rocky beach at Welcombe Mouth. It's a magnificent piece of coastline. Henna Cliff, passed on Point ⑤, is the highest sheer cliff in England after Beachy Head in Sussex and, in complete contrast, from here you get a clear view of the hideous satellite tracking station, sticking out like a sore thumb from its clifftop position south towards Bude. But it's a real treat to come and explore this part of the coast, where the dramatic scenery and weather conditions constantly remind you of just how insignificant you are compared to the natural elements.

Morwenstow and the Revd RS Hawker

The remote hamlet of Morwenstow, 2 miles (3.2km) from the Devon border, really is in the middle of nowhere. It is a fascinating place, best known for its connection with the eccentric 19th-century vicar, the Revd Robert Stephen Hawker. This colourful character came in 1834 and built the pinnacled rectory, to replace the former derelict building, next to the church. He was a drug addict throughout his life, and spent many hours meditating in his hut on the cliff edge, where he also wrote poetry. Some say he also used to keep an eye out for potential disasters at sea, common along this coast, and gave every shipwreck victim a Christian burial. This eccentric figure is said to have worn a fisherman's jumper over his priestly robes, knitted in a pattern specific to Morwenstow, and seaman's boots. He is believed to have introduced the harvest festival service, and wrote the famous *Shall Trelawny Die?*, an inspiring Cornish ballad. He died in 1875, having converted to Catholicism on his death bed.

The Church of St Morwenna & St John the Baptist is the most northerly parish church in Cornwall, and occupies a striking position just inland from Vicarage Cliff. Its pinnacled tower is clearly visible from the coast path and provided a useful landmark. There is a Saxon font, and evidence of the original Norman building in the three arches, with zig-zag moulding, in the north arcade. The church was enlarged and restored during the 16th and 17th centuries, and there is lots of fine wood carving in the roof, pews and bench endings.

Walk 47 Directions

① Walk left up the coast path. Cross two stiles, then walk down to **Marsland Mouth** and cross **Marsland Water** into Cornwall.

② Follow coast path markers inland, then turn right and up onto **Marsland Cliff**. The path runs along the cliff, down very steep steps into a combe, over a small bridge, then up the other side (**Cornakey Cliff**). Proceed along the edge of the field, crossing four stiles before dropping steeply down into a combe via a footbridge/stile. Walk up the other side to gain the top of **Henna Cliff**.

③ At the next stile, where there is a metal seat, turn left inland, keeping the wire fence right. At the bank at the field end turn right; then turn left through two gates and walk straight across the next field towards **Westcott Farm**.

WHAT TO LOOK FOR ⓘ

As you drop down towards Marsland Mouth at Point ①, pause to look at the little stone hut by the path. This is attributed to the poet and playwright Ronald Duncan (1914–82), and you'll find fresh water from a local well inside. If you go straight past the churchyard on your way back to the main route after Point ④, you can follow footpath signs to the coast path. Just to the south of this you'll find **Hawker's Hut**, a wooden turf-roofed construction, originally built of driftwood, nestling just over the cliff edge, with superb views out to sea.

---

④ At the hedge break before the farm turn right, downhill. Pass through a hedge gap towards a footpath sign. Enter the wood and climb over a stile/footbridge. Walk uphill past the vicarage, then cross over a stone stile into the graveyard. Turn right towards the church, then left and left again to exit via the lychgate. Go straight ahead up the lane to find the **Bush Inn** right.

⑤ Return to the hedge break approaching **Westcott Farm** at Point ④. Go straight on uphill, following signs 'Alternative path avoiding farm'. Cross the next bank over wooden steps. Turn immediately right and go through an open gateway at the top right of that field (following yellow arrows).

WHERE TO EAT AND DRINK ⓘ

The **Rectory Tearooms** opposite the church are open daily, 11AM–6PM, from Easter to October, and serve a range of snacks and light lunches. October opening is reduced, depending on the weather. They aren't licensed, but Sunday lunch fans may take their own wine. The atmospheric **Bush Inn** was originally a monks' resthouse, parts date back to AD 950. It's a free house with bar snacks available at lunch times (not Sundays).

Turn left through a gate and cross the field. Climb over a stile, and walk round a small barn (right). A yellow arrow ahead directs you through a gate and down the drive to a concrete road.

⑥ Turn left towards **Cornakey Farm** and follow 'Alternative path avoiding farmyard' signs through a gate right. Turn left through a gate, then down steps. Turn right into a green lane.

⑦ At the next gate, arrows direct you along the bank (right). Pass through a gate and walk diagonally across the field, downhill. Cross the hedgebank via steps and go straight over the field. Cross a stile into a wooded area then go steeply down to cross a footbridge and up, out of the wood on a path. Follow arrows (right) over an grassy area before **Marsland Manor**. Pass through a line of trees, then go right and follow signs to a stile onto a lane.

⑧ Turn left; a few paces on turn left again (signed 'Marsland Mouth') on a track. Go through a gate and downhill. At a cottage on the right, keep left following marker posts to regain the coast path. Continue straight on to cross the stream into Devon and retrace your steps home.

Around Hartland Point

A long, rewarding walk along the coast path overlooking the island of Lundy.

•DISTANCE•	8¾ miles (14.1km)
•MINIMUM TIME•	5hrs 30min
•ASCENT / GRADIENT•	328ft (100m) ▲▲▲
•LEVEL OF DIFFICULTY•	🚶 🚶 🚶
•PATHS•	Coast path through fields; country lanes, 35 stiles
•LANDSCAPE•	Rugged coastline, farmland and wooded valleys
•SUGGESTED MAP•	aqua3 OS Explorer 126 Clovelly & Hartland
•START / FINISH•	Grid reference: SS 259245
•DOG FRIENDLINESS•	Dogs should be kept under control at all times
•PARKING•	Car park in centre of Hartland village
•PUBLIC TOILETS•	Near car park and in Stoke village

BACKGROUND TO THE WALK

Although this walk is a little longer – and harder – than all the others in this book, it's a must for anyone who wants to explore all parts of the county properly. The section of countryside to the east of the A39 Bude to Bideford road is often ignored by tourist guides, and little explored – and that's exactly why it is so wonderful. The village of Hartland was described by a traveller in the 1790s as having 'an air of poverty that depresses it to a level with a Cornish borough' – a pretty tough criticism – but you do get the impression that life in this remote corner of Devon has been hard.

Hartland Point and Lundy Island

Devon's north west tip is characterised by an extraordinary change in the nature of the coast. The cliffs along the coast from Clovelly, to the east, although high, are relatively calm and flat-topped, yet turn the corner at Hartland lighthouse and you enter a different world, where the craggy rocks on the seabed run in jagged parallel lines towards the unforgiving cliffs. You can understand why this area is peppered with shipwrecks. The coast path to the south of the point traverses over what is, in effect, a mass of vertical tiltings and contortions, caused by lateral pressure on the earth's crust around 300 million years ago. Hartland means 'stag island', although the area is a peninsula, and the feeling of space and remoteness is made even stronger by the fact that on a clear day there are inviting views of Lundy island, rising majestically out of the sea 10 miles (16km) offshore. On stormy days, when the wind is so strong you can barely stand, Lundy mysteriously disappears into a blanket of mist and spray. The island is basically a great lump of flat-topped granite, 52 million years old, 450ft (137m) high, 3 miles (4.8km) long and only ½ mile (800m) wide.

Extraordinary Hartland Quay dates back to 1586, when its building was authorised by Act of Parliament. Cargoes of coal, lime and timber were landed here, and in 1616 lead was brought in for repairs to the roof of St Nectan's Church at Stoke. The quay was active until 1893, and once abandoned was soon destroyed by the ravages of the sea. The buildings, including the stables for the donkeys that carried goods up the cliff in those times, have now been converted into the Hartland Quay Hotel, museum and shop. You still get a terrific sense of how tough life must have been here for the harbour master and his staff.

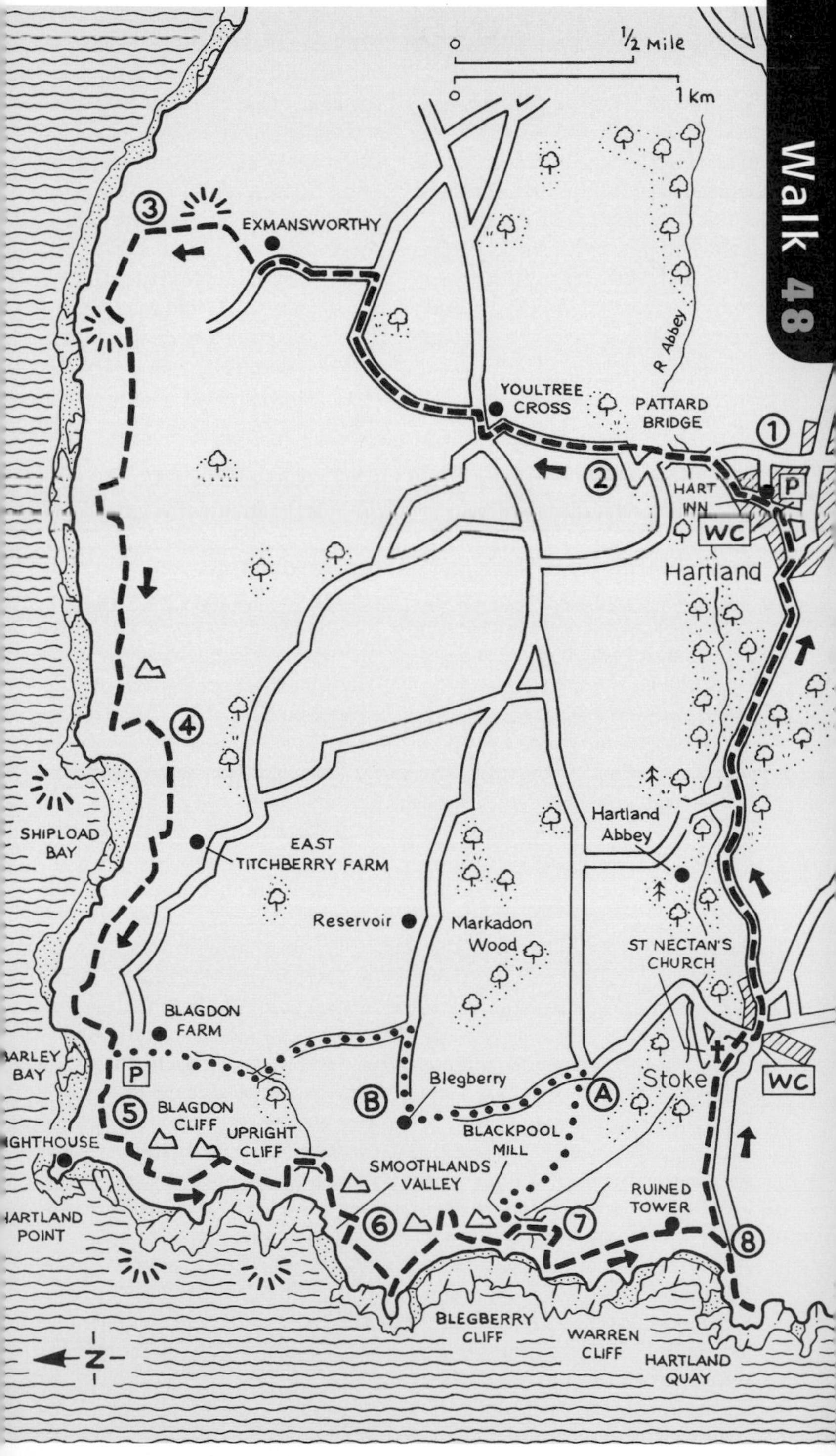

½ mile

1 km

③

EXMANSWORTHY

YOULTREE CROSS

PATTARD BRIDGE

R Abbey

①

②

HART INN

P

WC

Hartland

④

SHIPLOAD BAY

EAST TITCHBERRY FARM

Reservoir

Markadon Wood

Hartland Abbey

ST NECTAN'S CHURCH

BLAGDON FARM

MARLEY BAY

P

⑤

BLAGDON CLIFF

UPRIGHT CLIFF

Ⓑ

Blegberry

Ⓐ

BLACKPOOL MILL

Stoke

WC

LIGHTHOUSE

HARTLAND POINT

SMOOTHLANDS VALLEY

⑥

⑦

RUINED TOWER

⑧

BLEGBERRY CLIFF

WARREN CLIFF

HARTLAND QUAY

N

Walk 48

Walk 48 Directions

① Leave the car park past the **Hart Inn** (right) and turn right down **North Street**. Turn left down a narrow lane signposted 'Hartland Point'. Pass **Pattard Bridge** then follow the lane right. Just past a lane to the right, take the footpath sign right up steps and over a stile. Walk up the field and cross over the bank to rejoin the lane.

② Turn right and right again at **Youltree Cross**. A few steps on turn left at **Moor Cross**, signposted 'Exmansworthy'. The lane veers right; take the next lane left. Pass **Exmansworthy Farm**; turn right through the car park onto a grassy path, then cross a stile following signs 'Coast Path' to join a green lane. This ends at a stile into open fields. Follow the sign left, then go straight ahead to the coast path.

WHILE YOU'RE THERE ⓘ

Hartland Abbey, in a sheltered valley and passed on Point ⑧, dates from 1157, and has been a family home since 1539. The delightful gardens were designed by Gertrude Jekyll and the woodland walk, leading to a spectacular cove, is particularly lovely in spring.

---

③ Go left over a stile and continue over six stiles, then right downhill. Keep to the field edge to cross another stile. Go steeply downhill, and up over another stile. Cross two more stiles to reach **Shipload Bay**.

④ Follow the coast path through a gate and on past signs left to **Titchberry**. Walk on to cross six more stiles. Turn right towards the sea, pass round a gate then between the fence and cliff, to the right of the radar tower, to **Barley Bay**.

⑤ Follow coast path signs for **Hartland Quay** (the lighthouse is closed to the public). Take the narrow, concrete path leading steeply left, then left again along the field edge (**Blagdon Cliff**) and over a stile. Walk round the next stile and on above **Upright Cliff**. Cross over a stile and descend steeply into a combe then round a stile. Cross the stream via a stile/footbridge/stile. Steep steps lead up the other side to a stile. Turn right and follow coast path signs right over a stile into **Smoothlands valley**.

⑥ Climb steeply out of **Smoothlands** onto **Blegberry Cliff**. Walk down steep wooden steps into the next combe and cross the stream via a kissing gate, then up the other side and over a stile. Cross the next stile and descend to the combe at **Blackpool Mill**. Pass the cottage on the right.

⑦ Turn right to cross the stream on a bridge. Cross a stile and turn right onto **Warren Cliff** through a gate. Pass the ruined tower and at the gate ahead turn right for **Hartland Quay**, if you want a break.

⑧ Turn left inside the hedge. At the field end cross a stile and go straight on. Leave the field over a stile and walk past the cottages. Go through a kissing gate and stile, then another, to enter **St Nectan's** churchyard. Leave it via the lychgate and go straight on to follow the road back to **Hartland village**.

WHERE TO EAT AND DRINK ⓘ

Hartland has a range of pubs. Try the **Hart Inn**, the **Anchor** or the **King's Arms**. You can also get fish and chips in the square. There's a refreshment kiosk at Barley Bay. The **Hartland Quay Hotel** is a dramatic place to watch the ocean.

A Slightly Easier Way to View Lundy

A shorter, but still demanding, Hartland Point experience.
See map and information panel for Walk 48

•**DISTANCE**•	4 miles (6.4km)
•**MINIMUM TIME**•	2hrs
•**ASCENT / GRADIENT**•	180ft (50m) ▲▲▲
•**LEVEL OF DIFFICULTY**•	🚶 🚶 🚶

Walk 49 Directions (Walk 48 option)

If 8¾ miles (14.4km) terrifies you, try this shorter alternative, which still takes in the magnificent coastline south of Hartland Point – but remember – no coast path walks in this part of Devon are easy!

It's difficult to offer a reduced version of Walk 48, so this alternative starts from the lighthouse car park at **Blagdon Farm** (grid ref 235274). This means that you follow Walk 48 from Point ⑤ (**Barley Bay**) to the end of Point ⑥, but do not turn right after **Blackpool Mill** cottage: keep straight on up the track, heading inland (signs to '**Berry**').

At a red metal gate ('private') turn sharp left up a narrow hedged path then over a stile onto open cliffs. Where the gorse on the right narrows, take a tiny path right into the open field, then right inland to join a farm track. The rocky track leaves the next field via a metal gate. As **Berry** is approached there are wonderful views right of the 14th-century church at **Stoke**. The track meets a lane via a stile/gate on a

sharp bend at Point Ⓐ; turn immediately left down a green lane (permissive path). The lane runs downhill – then up to **Blegberry**.

When a cottage appears through the hedge right, veer right away from the wall to join the cottage drive, and up to a T-junction of lanes (the farmyard is left). Turn right (Point Ⓑ); after 200yds (183m) turn left down a green lane, signed '**To public bridleway**'. This becomes narrow, muddy and rocky, runs steeply downhill to cross a stream on a footbridge, then follows the stream briefly.

Where the stream veers left, pass through a gate and ahead to a footpath post. Turn right, following the bridleway to **Blagdon** uphill, through a gate and on to the farmyard. Go up the drive (house right) straight on and downhill to your car.

WHAT TO LOOK FOR ⓘ

Look out for **Lundy** – best seen from the cliffs near the lighthouse. You can take a boat from either Bideford or Ilfracombe, on a day trip. Every journey to the island is tinged with the added edge that the weather conditions might not let you get there at all or, of course, get home again.

Walk 50

The Far West – Along the Two Castles Trail

From Lifton near the Cornish border to secluded Stowford.

•DISTANCE•	6½ miles (10.4km)
•MINIMUM TIME•	3hrs
•ASCENT / GRADIENT•	165ft (50m)
•LEVEL OF DIFFICULTY•	
•PATHS•	Fields, green lanes and country lanes
•LANDSCAPE•	Undulating farmland and wooded river valleys
•SUGGESTED MAP•	aqua3 OS Explorer 112 Launceston & Holsworthy
•START / FINISH•	Grid reference: SS 387851
•DOG FRIENDLINESS•	Dogs to be kept under control at all times
•PARKING•	On Fore Street (the old A30) opposite post office in Lifton
•PUBLIC TOILETS•	Lifton village, and Dingles Steam Village

Walk 50 Directions

Lifton, just 4 miles (6.4km) from the Cornish border, is a somewhat unprepossessing place. It seems to have suffered from its time fronting the old A30, for many years the main route into Cornwall, and you get the feeling that it's still recovering from the aftermath of traffic overload. Yet the Two Castles Trail, a long-distance walking route that runs between the Norman castles at Launceston and

Okehampton (both worth a visit), passes through the village, and within minutes you can lose yourself in that remote and little-visited strip of green, rolling countryside that lies between the new and old A30 routes.

Cross over **Fore Street** to walk down **North Road** (by the **Lifton Hall Hotel**). Follow the lane past the primary school to reach **Glendale Nursery**, and turn left before the nursery car park. Follow the lane gently uphill until you see a public bridleway sign through a gate right. Turn right, and follow the edge of the field (hedge left) until you see a bridge over the **River Wolf** across the field; cut right to cross the river. The Wolf was dammed in 1990 to form **Roadford Lake**, to the north of the A30. It's a lovely spot, with a gift shop and tea room, and excellent sporting facilities and footpaths.

Follow the well-signed track, through woodland, uphill away

WHILE YOU'RE THERE

Go and see **Okehampton Castle**, which lies at the Devon end of the Two Castles Trail and is a great place to explore. Once one of the largest castles in the county, and home of the Earls of Devon in medieval times, the substantial ruins include the Norman motte and the remains of the keep, as well as the 14th-century hall. As an added bonus the castle, managed by English Heritage, enjoys a delightful setting with woodland walks and a riverside picnic area.

from the river. It leads into a broad green lane, which bends sharp left and continues slightly uphill to pass the entrance to the car park at **Dingles Steam Village**. Join the tarmac lane to pass the café and buildings of **Dingles** at **Milford Farm** (left). This 'celebration of working steam in the countryside' is open 10:30AM–5:30PM daily (except Fridays), Easter to 31 October. There are marked footpaths along the banks of the **Thrushel** and **Wolf** rivers signed off the trail here. The lane ends at a road (**Hayne Bridge** to the right). Turn left and walk uphill until you see a gritty track (signed '**Public bridleway**') right.

Turn right to pass **Arracott** (right) and go through a gate onto a straight green lane, which ends at another gate. Turn right through a gate to enter a plantation of young indigenous trees. The path runs downhill to the bottom corner of the field – if you look sharp left you get a good view of the Gothic mansion at **Hayne**, rebuilt in 1810, and the seat of the Harris family from the reign of Henry VIII until 1864. There are some splendid 18th-century monuments to members of the family in Stowford

church. The path leads through a group of huge beeches and oaks, to emerge by a white cottage (left). Carry on down the drive to meet the lane opposite **Lamerton Foxhound kennels**.

Turn right to cross the **River Thrushel** on **Stowford Bridge**, then turn steeply uphill to find the beautiful, secret **Church of St John the Baptist** (left). Dating from the 14th century, this was restored in 1874 by Sir George Gilbert Scott, architect of St Pancras station, at a cost of £4,000. He was involved in restoration work at Exeter Cathedral at the time. The 19th-century interior woodwork (copied from earlier examples) is said to be some of the finest in England. Look out for the wonderful views towards Cornwall, and the 1770 sundial over the door. Don't miss the inscribed Stowford Stone, found by the entrance to the churchyard, believed to date from the 6th or 7th centuries.

To continue on to the **Royal Exchange**, leave the church and walk on through the village, past the village hall (left) keeping to the main lane, to pass the **Stowford House Hotel**. Just over ¼ mile (400m) on you will reach the old A30. Turn right for the pub.

Walking in Safety

All these walks are suitable for any reasonably fit person, but less experienced walkers should try the easier walks first. Route finding is usually straightforward, but you will find that an Ordnance Survey map is a useful addition to the route maps and descriptions.

Risks

Although each walk here has been researched with a view to minimising the risks to the walkers who follow its route, no walk in the countryside can be considered to be completely free from risk. Walking in the outdoors will always require a degree of common sense and judgement to ensure that it is as safe as possible.

- Be particularly careful on cliff paths and in upland terrain, where the consequences of a slip can be very serious.

- Remember to check tidal conditions before walking on the seashore.

- Some sections of route are by, or cross, busy roads. Take care and remember traffic is a danger even on minor country lanes.

- Be careful around farmyard machinery and livestock, especially if you have children with you.

- Be aware of the consequences of changes in the weather and check the forecast before you set out. Carry spare clothing and a torch if you are walking in the winter months. Remember the weather can change very quickly at any time of the year, and in moorland and heathland areas, mist and fog can make route finding much harder. Don't set out in these conditions unless you are confident of your navigation skills in poor visibility. In summer remember to take account of the heat and sun; wear a hat and carry spare water.

- On walks away from centres of population you should carry a whistle and survival bag. If you do have an accident requiring the emergency services, make a note of your position as accurately as possible and dial 999.

Acknowledgements

From the author
This book is dedicated to Mum, who would have been so pleased, and to Dad.

It has been a privilege (and a huge amount of fun!) to be given an excuse to explore the county in such depth. I am really grateful to all those long-suffering friends, and my two sons Nick and Joffy, who assisted me in so many ways, from giving me ideas and support, and accompanying me on walks, to reminding me to switch off the pause button on the dictaphone (and helping me sort out left from right!) – so thank you so much to Brenda, Carol, Ced, Christine, Emma, Jane, John, Les, Steve, Susanne and, last but certainly not least, to Terry.

Series management: Outcrop Publishing Services, Cumbria
Series editor: Chris Bagshaw
Front cover: AA Photo Library/A Lawson